Katherine Lost

Charlene A. Ryan

PROLOGUE

MONDAY

Katherine climbed the stairs with lead feet and a heavy heart. Her thoughts were fuzzy and she had the odd sensation of watching her life unfold from a distance. Muffled voices rose from the kitchen below—her dad asking, 'how did it go?', her mom saying, 'give her a minute,' Declan grumbling 'can we eat now?'. But the sounds were hollow and faraway. She could smell the sausage pizza and butterscotch brownies even from upstairs, and although she knew she must be hungry, Katherine couldn't eat.

Arriving at her room, she flipped the 'KATHERINE'S PLACE' sign over so it now read 'DO NOT DISTURB!' Closing the door firmly, she picked up her oversized unicorn stuffie and crawled into bed. As she wrapped herself around the unicorn and pulled the blankets up to her chin, the sense of unreality shifted into something more akin to grief. This day was supposed to end much differently. How did it go so wrong?

CHAPTER ONE

THE END

MONDAY

Monday morning had started like almost any other. Mrs. Keyes was buzzing around the house, checking that everyone was up and doing what they needed to get out the door clean, fed, dressed, on time, and with everything they needed for the day. Mr. Keyes was tethered to his desk, finishing yet another late-night into early-morning project. Declan and Addison were fighting over bathroom time, and Mia was cuddling Moe, listening to Katherine practice.

The youngest child, Mia loved to sit under the baby grand while the sounds emanating from above washed over and around her. It was probably not the safest place in the world for her to hang out, but it was her favorite. While the older siblings didn't pay much notice to their 12-year-old sister's never-ending piano playing, Mia was entranced by Katherine's music and could sit there for hours with her eyes serenely closed, taking it all in.

"Mia, come and eat your breakfast, please—your pancakes are getting cold."

The Keyes were the only family Katherine knew that routinely had pancakes on school days. But mom's trick of baking one giant pancake and cutting it into individual squares made *oven pancakes* an easy morning offering. Mia snapped back to reality, crawled out from her sonorous nook, and left her sister alone with the dog and the piano.

Starting at the beginning again, Katherine's nimble fingers moved over the keys as if with a mind of their own. She'd played this piece so many times there was no longer any need to think, only to feel. And so she did. She felt the power of the music, the intensity of emotion, and the strength and vulnerability of the song within her.

"Katherine!" her mother called out, cutting through her reverie, "I'm going now with your sisters and brother. I have to stop at the office for a minute, but I should be back in about an hour and then we'll go, ok? Make sure you eat something."

Katherine finished the piece she was playing, closed the lid, and went into the kitchen to see what food she could find that wouldn't require any actual effort on her part. Popping a couple of pancake squares into the toaster, she poured a glass of chocolate milk and waited for them to crisp up the way she liked. Then, with a crossword open on her phone, she sat down to breakfast and focused her attention on searching for words that vaguely resembled the definitions offered. It was frustrating and, for the most part, fruitless, but the exercise served its purpose—this was not a moment to be left alone with her thoughts.

Done with breakfast, she went to the bathroom to finish

getting ready. With Declan and Addison gone, Katherine now had time to fully consider her look without "hurry up" pressure from her teenage siblings. Cueing her favorite band up on her phone, she proceeded to brush her teeth then her golden brown hair, pulling it back off her face and securing it with a sparkly clip. She examined her deep brown eyes and light olive skin, and wondered whether the occasion might call for makeup, then decided against it. Turning to the full-length mirror, she checked her outfit. It was definitely more dressed-up than she would normally wear to school, but not so dressed up as to look like full-on performance attire—it was morning, after all, and not *technically* a performance. Satisfied with what she saw, she took a deep breath, smiled at her reflection, and went back to the piano to play.

***

It took 40 minutes to get there, thanks to a fender-bender that brought traffic to a stand-still for what felt like forever. Katherine was thankful that they'd left in plenty of time, but any buffer was gone by the time they'd parked and made their way into the building. *The Valley View School for the Performing Arts.* Katherine's dream school. She pinched herself.

Check-in was in the main foyer, a big open space with tiered wooden floors and glass walls flanked by floor-to-ceiling red velvet curtains. It looked like a stage. In her mind's eye, Katherine could see the performances as vividly as if they were real. She could see herself in them…

A registration table was set up front and center, with three students several years older than Katherine—*maybe seniors?* —taking names, handing out welcome bags, and directing prospective 7th graders to where they needed to go. "Welcome to *Valley View!*" the girl in the center said with a bright smile. *A dancer.* Katherine couldn't quite put her finger on how she knew this, but something about the way she sat and moved reminded her of her friend, Maren. And for the first time, she wondered briefly why Maren wasn't there with her today.

Quickly scanning the schedule, she soon found herself moving out of the foyer and further into the building, following the students' directions—down the hallway, last door on the right—to the room designated for her first test. *Aural skills*, not Katherine's favorite, by any stretch of the imagination. Passing classrooms with pianos and drums and music playing on sound systems, she tried not to get distracted. But her need to study there was growing by the minute.

Arriving at the test room, Katherine grabbed a pencil and handed her bag to her mom. She entered through a back door, took a seat, pulled the desk arm down, then surveyed the room. A dozen or so kids—looking around, fidgeting, finger drumming— waited anxiously for the test to begin. Katherine wondered if she knew any of them. It was hard to tell from the backs of their heads, but she didn't think so.

Before long, test papers were handed out and all heads bent over them. Katherine sent up a silent prayer, then focused her attention on the sounds ringing out from the piano up front. Panic began to niggle around the edges of her mind as she worked to decipher the intervals, melodies, harmonies, and rhythms. But there was no time for panic now. She forced it away, determined to not let fear keep her from her dream. With a clear mind and ears working on overdrive, the answers seemed obvious. And by the time this first assessment was over and she laid her pencil down, Katherine began to relax in the hope that the rest of the day would go as well.

A student assistant led the way to the next test, offering a guided tour along the way. "These are the practice rooms with pianos; practice rooms without pianos are directly above us. Here's the main office. Teachers' studios are down that hallway. This is a rehearsal room. Those are the lockers for big instruments…"

The tour ended abruptly as they arrived at their destination. "And… here we are!" he said, bowing and waving his arm with a dramatic flourish—a dead give-away that this kid was in the school's acting stream.

A row of chairs lined the walls up and down the hallway. *Was there a row like this outside the last test room?* Katherine couldn't remember—it seemed like ages ago. Processing the sign that was thumb-tacked to the door, her heart began to race, and she realized in that moment that there were worse tests than aural skills yet to come. *Sight-reading Assessments.*

Katherine was an admitted perfectionist. She knew it, her friends and family and teacher knew it. She loved learning to play challenging pieces, and happily practiced each section over and over again, in private, until it was just right. Sight reading went against every fiber of her being. The whole prospect of attempting new pieces in front of an examiner was just wrong, in her opinion. Trying to play them through from beginning to end without stopping to figure the parts out properly was her version of torture. And it was up next.

With only one of the day's roster of tests done, and a worse one looming behind that thumb-tacked door, Katherine tried hard to focus on the lovely red velvet curtains and foyer that felt like a stage. She'd need to hold onto that sense of awe and excitement as the day went on, to remind her of how much she wanted to go here. Because the actual audition was looming, and the butterflies in her stomach knew it.

CHAPTER TWO

THE NOTE

TUESDAY

For as long as Katherine could remember, her life had centered around the piano. She played for hours each day, every day, without being asked or reminded—she just did it. And she *loved* it. The obsession began in second grade and, looking back, it was hard to know whether she had desperately wanted to play the piano or just really wanted to do what her friends were doing. In any case, Katherine asked her mom if she could sign up for lessons, too, and she continued to ask every day until her mom took the hint that she wasn't going to stop until she actually did try it. At first, Mrs. Keyes registered her daughter not with her beloved Mrs. Bellamy, but with a young teacher she found through the local college's student ads. They didn't even have a piano at first—just an old electric organ—but the Keyes didn't want to invest in a piano unless this seemed like it might be more than just a passing fancy. It was, and so they soon upgraded to a second-hand upright, and then a better one, and finally to the beautiful new baby grand that she had now. Katherine loved each instrument even more than the last, but this newest acquisition had stolen her heart. She still couldn't believe it was hers. It was the kind of thing she'd expect kids from much wealthier families to have. But mom and dad were the kind of parents who scrimped and saved and did whatever it took to give their children what they needed. And Mrs. Bellamy said that Katherine was getting to a level where she needed a good instrument—this one, in fact. So they made it happen.

Katherine spent most of her out-of-school time at the piano. She wasn't interested in either playing sports or watching other people play them, so afterschool and weekends were largely dedicated to her music. Not that she was a recluse or anything— her three best friends made sure of that. Maren, Naomi, and Bridget had been tight since they'd met in first grade. They all had their own talents and interests, but none were into music like she was. Which was probably a good thing, Katherine thought— they kept her balanced. She had music friends, too, and although they didn't spend time together outside of school, they connected at band practice and sometimes at lunch. Charlotte, Mariana, and Aaliyah were as into music as she was, and they were always eager to talk about this shared interest. Katherine enjoyed her two friend worlds—one that was all about music and one that was anything but.

On normal days when Katherine had a performance or competition, she kept this information to herself. It was better, she found, to perform without the pressure of expectation from her friends. The thought of everyone asking, '*How did it go?*' was unnerving, so she usually didn't mention her performance life at all. While a tiny piece of her wished she could share the stress and anticipation with her friends, not having to face that question or feel the weight of their good-wishes-stress was more than worth keeping it to herself. Which made this day particularly trying. *Everyone*—or at least her three best friends—knew she was auditioning for *Valley View*. The reminder had popped up on her phone the day before when Bridget was scrolling through her pictures, so of course the whole group was immediately informed. The 'good luck', 'break a leg', and 'you got this' texts on Monday morning had been just about all she could bear.

What was she going to do? How could she possibly relive yesterday's trauma, only to see the disbelief and sympathy on her friends' faces? Maybe she should just be sick today, and tomorrow, and, well—maybe for the rest of the week. Then her friends might be too worried about her health to bother about the audition. But Katherine couldn't lie. She'd tried. And every time she did, the untruth stuck in her throat like the grass that Moe happily chewed and immediately regretted every time he grazed the backyard. No, she'd have to come clean. And the very thought brought her despair to a whole new level.

***

Katherine arrived at school just in time for the bell. Most kids had already made their way to class, with just a few stragglers still exiting cars and locking up bikes.

"Have a great day, Katherine!" She could see her mom's smile without even looking up. "And remember what Anne always says…"

Anne of Green Gables was one of her favorite books, and whenever Katherine had a particularly lousy day, Mrs. Keyes reminded her of Anne's mantra that *'Today is a new day with no mistakes in it yet.'* Somehow, waking up and leaving the house this morning seemed to have already been a mistake, but Katherine didn't want to get into it, so she grunted a "Bye, mom" and reluctantly made her way into the building and down the hallway to her first class.

Mr. Ryan had already started to teach, and she was able to slip in without any opportunity for questions from well-meaning friends. Her phone had been dinging incessantly since early this morning, but she refused to check it and instead had taken the extreme and rare action of turning it off and hiding it in the bottom of her bag.

As her teacher prattled on about ratios and percentages, Katherine's mind wandered. Her eyes fixed on the waving branches of the weeping willow outside, and she found herself thinking about what might make a tree weep—and then about the fact that she had something in common with a tree. At least on the inside.

A quick rush of movement caught the corner of her eye. Looking down, she saw on the floor a small folded piece of paper with her name scrawled on top.

The moment she'd been dreading.

Bridget and Naomi were both sitting close enough to have sent it, but they were facing Mr. Ryan and gave no indication of doing anything other than listening to their teacher. Katherine held her breath as she bent down to pick it up.

"Katherine?" Mr Ryan's voice rang in her ears.

Oh God.

Please don't let him read it out loud. If history was any indication, he'd make her respond in front of the whole class. *Why, oh why did she come to school today??*

"What is the reduced form of 30:35?"

What? Oh—math! She slid her foot on top of the paper, looked up to the sky, as she often did when she was thinking, and answered. That was a close one. For the rest of the period, she didn't dare reach for the note. Math seemed to go on forever and she wished she could slump over and hang her head like her willow soul mate outside.

Finally, the bell rang and snapped her to attention. Making her way to the door, she remembered the note and circled back to collect it. By the time she got to the hallway, Naomi and Bridget had both disappeared into the sea of students. Losing herself in the swarm, she tucked the paper into her bag and headed to her next class.

With an audible sigh, Katherine remembered that none of her close friends were in her English section, which meant she had at least 50 minutes without the threat of having to talk about things looming over her. Taking a seat in the back of the room, she closed her eyes and waited for Mrs. Martin to get started. This was the kind of moment she would normally use to think about her music—which was weird, she knew, but she loved to hear her pieces and found she could do so in her mind just as well as on the piano. Today, though, she just couldn't face it. And the prospect, combined with yesterday's disaster, came crashing down, leaving her feeling even more miserable than she had all morning. Another mistake. So much for Anne and her lousy mantra!

Today was not going to be her day.

CHAPTER THREE
THE QUESTIONS
TUESDAY

Did anyone know?

Crouching in the back corner of the band room, Katherine retrieved her instrument from its velvety case and tried to remember if she had told her music friends about the audition. *Did anyone else here try out?* These would have been good things to think about last night, or during English or Math, but with rehearsal starting she didn't have a moment more to reflect.

It was a busy class. With graduation and end-of-year concerts looming, there was still a fair bit of ground to cover—which, frankly, was a relief. With no down-time, there was also no opportunity to obsess over yesterday. And the first trumpet parts in all the current pieces were busy and exciting and fun, so at least there was that.

At the end of class, Mrs. Gibbons asked to see her. *Oh no.*

Mrs. Gibbons was her favorite teacher and an awesome musician. She really didn't want to discuss her recent failure with her. *How did she even find out?*

"Katherine," she said, "I know you try to focus on trumpet at school and keep your piano life more private…".

Here we go…

"But one of the pieces the choir is doing for graduation has a really complicated accompaniment and Mr. Bertulli needs a strong pianist for it. He has other students for the rest of the songs, but would you consider helping out with this one? I told him I'd ask."

Uh. What? This was definitely not what she had expected.

"Oh, um, sure. Okay. Thanks for thinking of me."

"Well, Katherine, you're an excellent pianist. I've heard you play." She smiled at Katherine, one of her star students who, embarrassed at the praise, suddenly took a keen interest in her shoes. "You know, Mrs. Bellamy is an old friend of mine. She says you are one of the most talented young pianists she's ever seen." Katherine shifted her feet as heat rushed to her face. Sensing her discomfort, Mrs. Gibbons finished up, "I know you're a private person, but extraordinary talent is hard to keep under wraps."

Katherine smiled shying as she accepted the sheet music and moved to put her trumpet away. It was nice to know that Mrs. Bellamy thought so highly of her, even if it was super uncomfortable to actually hear it. She'd known she was one of the better students, but her teacher played things close to the chest and held high expectations for everyone. It was one of the things Katherine loved about her—that she expected her students to be self-motivated and self-aware. But at this moment, when doubt had all but taken over, it sure helped to hear these unexpected words of encouragement.

And, it seemed, Mrs. Gibbons did not know about yesterday.

***

Katherine opened her lunch and rooted around. Her mom always snuck a treat in the bottom—a kind of reward for eating all of the more nutritious stuff above it. However, Mrs. Keyes never actually said that the healthy food had to be eaten first, or at all, so Katherine frequently ignored these expectations. If ever there was a day for chocolate, this was it.

Aaliyah, Mariana, and Charlotte were setting their guitars and amps up near the drum set. Waving hi, she removed her earbuds to listen. Katherine loved rock music, but she didn't know how to play it. Her piano repertoire was all classical—Bach and Mozart and those guys—which she loved, as well. But sometimes she imagined it would be cool to let go of all the rules and expectations and just rock out. Katherine wondered what Mrs. Bellamy would think. It was hard to know.

"Hey Kat!" the girl on electric guitar called out. "You play keys, right?"

"Ah, no—not really, Charlotte. I mean, I play piano, but like, classical music."

"You know scales and chords and stuff?"

"Yeah…" she answered, cautiously.

"Would you help us out? This song we're working on has a pretty important keyboard part and we don't have anyone to play it. Carl was going to, but he broke his wrist. Can you try it?"

Katherine froze momentarily. This was outside her comfort zone, but she couldn't say no to at least trying, in spite of her fear—that would just be rude. So instead, she retrieved her phone from the depths of her bag and turned it on to search for the song.

Determined to ignore the double digits on her text icon, she pushed down the panic, closed her eyes, and listened carefully. Charlotte was right—the keyboard part did seem pretty straightforward. She listened again, then moved to the keyboard and plugged it in. If anyone had told her before this very minute that she could do this, she probably wouldn't have believed them, but before long she had worked out the part and was playing along with the band. And she found that working through the song and putting it together with her friends was not nearly as scary as it had always seemed. Quite the opposite, actually—it was kind of fun, and exactly what she needed on this particular day that had been teetering between sadness and stress.

"Can you play with us again tomorrow?"

Charlotte's invitation echoed in Katherine's ears as she made her way to her afternoon classes feeling lighter than she had all day.

CHAPTER FOUR
THE PHONE
TUESDAY

Tuesday afternoon was relatively uneventful, and Katherine heaved a sigh of relief when the bell finally rang to go home. She had successfully managed to avoid her best friends and their text messages all day, and no one else seemed to be aware of either the fact that the audition had taken place or the horror that it had been. Lingering in her last class, she packed up slowly and stopped by the restroom on the way back to her locker. Not because she needed to go, but rather to drag out the end-of-day process in the hope that all would be calm and quiet as she made her way out of the building.

But the universe—or rather, her friends—had other plans. Maren, Bridget, and Naomi were waiting for her on the front steps. Katherine took a deep breath and pasted on a smile.

"Hey guys!" she said, a little too brightly. "I haven't seen you all day!"

"Yeah, we missed you at lunch. Did you have a rehearsal or something?" Bridget asked.

"Actually, weirdly, I did. It was a last-minute thing."

"We figured. Did you forget your phone? We've been texting all day."

"And you didn't answer my note," added Naomi.

Oh, jeez! Katherine had totally forgotten the note, which was currently stashed somewhere in the depths of her bag, alongside her powered-down phone.

"Yeah, sorry—I left my phone charging at home, and I totally forgot about the note."

Naomi was clearly hurt, and Katherine raced to explain, "Mr. Ryan threw me with his question. I thought he saw the note, and I didn't hear his question, and then I had to answer it. I was flustered and it slipped my mind. Should I read it now?" Katherine was anxious to make things right with her friend, but hoped that she'd say 'no'. Digging around in her bag right now was a risk.

"No, it's okay," said Naomi. "I just wanted to ask if you were free on Friday night. I was thinking of having a sleepover. Maren and Bridget can both come. You were the only one I hadn't been able to connect with yet."

Oh.

"Yeah—that would be awesome!" said Katherine. "I'm totally open. Definitely!"

The girls walked home together, chatting happily about the party. Before long, they began branching off to head toward their homes and only Bridget and Katherine were left. Bridget was Katherine's closest friend and she had a sometimes-annoying ability to read her mind.

"Is everything okay?" she asked quietly.

"Yeah—why?" Katherine responded.

"I don't know. You just seem a little off today. Is something bothering you?"

"No… no, I'm good. Just a little tired, I guess. But thanks for asking."

"Um, okay… But if you need to talk about anything, you know you can, right?"

"Yeah, I know—thanks, Bridge."

Bridget's house was on the same street as Katherine's, and they walked in silence until they got there.

"See you tomorrow, then. Or text me later if you want."

"Yeah, see you tomorrow—or tonight, maybe. We'll see."

She thought about Bridget's offer to talk. She obviously knew something was up, but Katherine just didn't want to get into it. Maybe tomorrow, or maybe never, but definitely not tonight. She felt bad keeping it from her friend, but she was super grateful that no one had asked her about yesterday.

****

"So, how did it go yesterday?"

Are you kidding? She had managed to avoid that question all day—only to arrive home and hear it from her 15-year-old brother who, as far as she could tell, barely knew she existed. *How had he not clued in last night when she didn't come down for her favorite dinner? Aargh!*

"Uh, fine," Katherine lied.

"Cool. So… can you babysit Mia on Friday?"

What?

"I told mom and dad I'd babysit, like, a month ago, but now Jamil's having a party and I really want to go. Can you babysit instead?"

"Sorry," she lied again. *Hmmm… she was getting better at this.* "Maren's having a sleepover on Friday and I already told her I could go. Did you ask Addison?"

"No, not yet. She's never free on the weekend." He grabbed a bowl and filled it with brownies. Not ready to give up yet, he thought out loud, "Maybe I can convince mom and dad to go out early so I can catch some of the party when they get back."

That seemed unlikely, but Katherine said, "Yeah, maybe," anyhow. "Good luck with it."

On normal days, Katherine would grab a snack and head straight for the piano. But today was not a normal day. She grabbed some cold pizza from the fridge and walked past the living room to her bedroom, looking straight ahead.

Opening her phone, she checked her socials and scrolled through some stories—still ignoring the texts—then put a show on Netflix. She wasn't supposed to watch T.V. while doing homework, but today she needed the distraction. Her mom would never believe her, but Katherine was convinced that it helped her to focus—especially when a storm of negative thoughts threatened to overtake her mind at any moment. When her work was done, she lay down on the bed. And fell asleep to the sound of her favorite show playing episode after episode after episode.

CHAPTER FIVE
THE SEARCH
WEDNESDAY

```
Charlotte: Do you know this song?
Charlotte: Can you try it?
Charlotte: Meet you at lunch
```

The dinging of new texts prompted Katherine to finally accept that it was morning. Opening her eyes to check her messages, she clicked on the link and watched a video from what looked like the '80s (the musicians looked like the kids in her mom's prom pictures). Deciding to ignore the questionable hair and wardrobe choices, she closed her eyes to listen. A rock ballad. It was beautiful.

Oh my gosh. Classical Kathy playing a rock ballad?! Declan's nickname flashed across her mind. Taking a deep breath, she closed her eyes and pressed *play* again. It took a moment to push away the self-doubt and just focus on the sounds, but when she did the piano part rang through loud and clear. *She could figure this out*, she thought with more than a little surprise.

Katherine made her way downstairs, and this time went to the piano. For a moment, a well of sadness threatened to overflow. But she needed to see if she could work out the song and this was the only way to do it. Shoving grief to the pit of her stomach, she sat down on the bench and pressed *play* yet again. The chords were simple enough, but which ones were they? Placing her hands on the keyboard, she began to work them out, each failed attempt bringing her closer to success. Katherine was exhilarated by the work. It felt good to use her ears and brain and hands in this way.

Thinking of Charlotte, Aaliyah, and Mariana, Katherine channeled the good vibes from yesterday's rehearsal. Playing and replaying the recording, intent on having it ready for today's session, she focused on finding the sounds on her own instrument. *Finally, a good use for those aural skills…* she thought. A flash of *Valley View* swept across her mind. *Don't go there, Katherine. Focus.*

A little light had switched on inside her. *A spark.* And regret would only snuff it out.

***

The morning passed quietly and without incident. No one asked about the audition, no one asked if she was ok, and no one mentioned music at all. A pop quiz in Math and a writing session in English meant quiet classes with little to no opportunity for social interaction. Then it was Art, which was always good. With everyone painting at their own easel, and calming new-age music floating around them, Katherine felt a kind of Zen. It was the perfect atmosphere for being in your own head with your own art.

They were working on abstract art this quarter, which she absolutely loved. The colors and shapes and freedom from constraints spoke to Katherine's soul. Connecting intensely with its openness and creative possibilities, she was deep in her zone when the bell rang.

In most other classes, she watched the clock, waiting impatiently for the bell to ring. Art was different, and Katherine found that it often rang too soon, startling her back to the real world. Normally she would take her time and linger over the last brush strokes. Today, though, she raced to clean up, then find a spot in the back of the 'in progress' area to safely store her work where it wouldn't be disturbed—she didn't have class again for two more days. Thankfully, they were working with oils now—a perk of sixth grade. Aside from the awesomeness of their vibrant colors, oil paints took longer to dry, which meant she could pick up where she left off pretty easily, building the layers up bit by bit. Ms. Flores was such a cool teacher and an awesome artist. *Playing with color* (quite possibly the best phrase ever uttered, in Katherine's opinion) was her favorite thing to do. The image so perfectly summed up exactly how she herself often felt. And next to music, there was nothing that gave Katherine such a sense of peace and fulfillment as working with a paintbrush.

***

Arriving at the band room later than planned, Katherine found to her surprise that she was the first one there. Dropping her stuff in the corner and fishing a treat out of the bottom of her lunch bag, she quickly set herself up at the keyboard to see what she could remember from this morning. Relieved that it was all still there, she played through the song a few more times to tighten it up and log it in her memory. With still no sign of any of the girls and the song now permanently etched in her head and hands, she found herself noodling while she waited—adding the occasional new note and messing with the rhythm to change up the overall feel. She'd probably have to play it the usual way when the band got there, but playing around this way was kind of fun.

If she could just work out the melody line now and add it to her part, she might even be able to turn this into a piece to play on her own without the band, if she wanted.

For the second time that day, a bell rang too soon, and Katherine reluctantly closed and unplugged the keyboard and pushed it back to its home against the wall. Grabbing her bag, she made her way to History, still caught up in the play of the last couple of hours, first with color and then with sound.

The thought almost stopped her in her tracks. *Oh wow!* She had never before realized two distinct realms of music making— the one where you *played music* and the one where you *played with music.* Her mind blown by the notion, she took her seat and responded 'here' when her name was called, but in reality, she was far away.

***

Katherine's mom picked her up directly from school. She had a dentist appointment, and in spite of her frequent requests, Mrs. Keyes seemed fundamentally opposed to scheduling visits during the school day. Today, though, Katherine was okay with it. Sure, she missed the after-school catch-up with her friends, but that meant one less opportunity for anyone to ask about Monday. Her phone dinged on the way there.

Charlotte: Sorry we couldn't meet at lunch Some kids were messing around during PE and Mr. Mac made us stay and run laps

Katherine: Ugh. PE is the WORST

Katherine: I worked out that song. Meet tomorrow?

Charlotte: Can't—Art Club. You're in it, too…

Katherine: Oh right. Friday?

Charlotte: Room's not free—jazz band

Katherine: Oh

Charlotte: What are you doing Saturday?

Katherine: Not much

Katherine: Want to come over?

Charlotte: What time?

Katherine: Afternoon? 3ish?

Charlotte: Send me your address

***

When Mr. Keyes got home from work, he found Katherine surrounded by storage bins in the garage. "What's going on,

Katherine?" he said. "Are you looking for something? Maybe I can help."

Katherine's dad was the Organizer-in-Chief of their family. Or at least he thought he was. He stuffed everything into bins—*everything*—whether the items belonged together or not – and then neatly stacked them on shelves around the walls of their double-car garage. Some were labelled (ambiguously) and some were not. Trying to find anything was like searching for a needle in the world's neatest haystack.

"Remember that electronic keyboard we used to have? Do we still have it?"

He paused for a second, "I think so. I remember Mom and I talked about donating it, but I think we decided to hang on to it instead, in case you might want to try it one day."

"Great. So, today's that day. Do you know where it is?"

"Maybe…" her dad replied. "Can you give me a minute to change and I'll help you look?"

It was pretty clean in the garage—no cars ever made it inside—so it was unlikely her dad would get dirty looking through these boxes. But Katherine knew he hated to stay in his business clothes once he was home. He felt it was hard to shift gears while still wearing a shirt with buttons on it.

"Alright. I'll grab a snack while you change."

Ten minutes and 3 mini chocolate-chip muffins later, Katherine returned to find her Dad already deep into the bins. "So, Katherine, this is new…" he said in a questioning voice. "What made you decide to track down the keyboard today?"

"Um, well—I've been playing a little bit of keyboard with some kids at school, and it's kind of cool. Plus, my friend,

Charlotte, is coming over to jam on the weekend and I'd rather use a keyboard than the piano. She plays electric guitar, so I think it would work better."

"Oh…" Her dad's surprise was hard not to notice. To his credit, he quickly recovered, adding, "That's awesome! I loved keyboard when I was your age. How long have you been playing with these kids?"

"Only once so far, but I think we're going to make it a regular thing. They've been sending me songs to work out."

"Really?" her dad said—again with the surprise. "What kind of music?"

"Like, these older rock songs. I don't know if the band does other stuff, too—they've been together for a while, I think. They needed a keyboard player for a song and asked me to fill in, so I don't really know a lot yet"

"Was it fun?" her dad asked. He was big on doing things that made you happy.

"Yeah, you know, it was," Katherine replied thoughtfully. It was too early to show him any major enthusiasm, in case she changed her mind or it didn't work out. "I never really played that kind of music before… or played piano with other people." She thought for a second, and added, "Or played music that I had to figure out just from listening to it…"

"Here it is!" her dad broke through her train of thought as he pulled the lid off an oversized bin that had been hidden under half a dozen others.

Katherine felt a tingle as they lifted the old DX-7 out of the bin. It wasn't too heavy, but it was awkward for one person to handle. So together they carried it to her bedroom and set it up on its stand. Anxious to give it a try privately, Katherine deflected her Dad's urge to reminisce with a quick "Thanks for your help, Dad!" and a peck on the cheek as she steered him toward the door. Grabbing her headphones from her desk, she plugged them in and sat down to play.

CHAPTER SIX
THE SLEEPOVER
THURSDAY AND FRIDAY

Katherine was unfocused. All Thursday she was just off—picturing herself, at random moments, right back on stage panicked and frozen, playing and replaying the scene over and over in her mind, increasingly regretting all possible thoughts and events that might have been at fault. And imagining all the ways it could have gone differently. Thursday was not a good day.

There was no specific reason for it. *It just wasn't.* It was one of those days when she really wished the world would leave her alone. She plodded along through her darkness, avoiding eye contact, and hoping not to run into any of her friends.

It was all so confusing, really. Last night had been great—really great—setting up the keyboard in her room and playing away happily for hours. There was no good reason she could put her finger on for how she felt today. Putting her head down, she pretended to read, but the same images kept reeling through her mind, and she was sad.

As long as Katherine could remember, she had wanted to go to *Valley View*. She had seen those kids perform at plenty of events, *even on TV*, and she wanted badly to be one of them. Imagine having time to practice and take lessons and learn all about music and performing *at school*—where every kid and teacher was just as into their art as she was! It was a dream, really. And she had desperately longed for it. *She still longed for it*, though it now haunted her and seemed out of reach. *Katherine was lost.*

It was bedtime before any light eked into her day. A stream of texts from Bridget.

```
Bridget: Can't wait for tomorrow night!
Bridget: Girls just wanna have fun
Bridget: Love you guys
Bridget: Besties rock
```

Katherine smiled weakly as she laid down her phone and decided that tomorrow would have to be a better day. *At least it had no mistakes in it—yet.*

***

Maybe she had just been tired. She tended towards darkness when she didn't sleep well. Or hungry? Ditto on the reaction front. But it was a vicious circle, she knew. When she felt down, she lost her appetite; and when she didn't eat, she felt down. Katherine tried to remember what she ate yesterday. *Did she eat yesterday?* She shook her head, couldn't remember. But whatever it was, hunger or exhaustion or something else entirely, by Friday morning the cloud had lifted, and she woke feeling positive and looking forward to seeing her friends.

Maren, Bridget, and Katherine converged on Naomi's house at 7pm, sleeping bags, pillows, and overnight kits in tow. They hadn't had a slumber party in ages and were excited to *just be together* for a whole night of uninterrupted fun. As she drove the crew to Naomi's, Katherine's mom said they would miss this when they grew up. But the girls were determined not to. *Why couldn't they have sleepovers when they were older?* There was no good reason they could think of. Even when they went away to college, they could get together when they came home for holidays. That way they would always be up on the news and they would never have to miss each other. They decided to make a pact.

The four friends had slumber parties down to an art, with a regular agreed-upon roster of activities. First, Pizza and Catch-up. Tonight, they decided to skip 'delivery' and make their own pizza (Naomi's mom's idea)—stretching the store-bought dough and everything. They were definitely not master pizza flippers, but it sure was fun to try.

Although they saw each other most days and texted regularly, there never seemed to be enough time during the week to hear everything that was going on. Pizza and Catch-up time ensured that everyone was up to date on each other's lives.

Next was Karaoke-Mani-Pedi—a strange hybrid activity born from the sheer boredom of waiting for painted nails to dry. It had been Bridget's idea many sleepovers ago, and the bizarre practice of singing dramatically to recorded background music while waving fresh manicures in the air stuck.

Last on the regular schedule was Popcorn and *GJWHF*. Popping the corn in an air popper, instead of microwave bags, they made it their own, largely by adding more melted butter and salt than could possibly be healthy for anyone. They always made two massive bowls before settling in for their favorite bonding movie, *Girls Just Wanna Have Fun*. Maren's mom had introduced it to them as one of her favorites from when she was young, and in spite of their initial wariness of anything that parents think is cool, they found that its storyline about music, dance, friendship, and fun resonated deeply. They watched it at every sleepover and before every school dance.

After the movie, the rest of the evening was always a bit of a 'free-for-all' —kind of the unstructured slumber party they imagined most kids had. The four friends chatted, talked about playing board games (but never did), snapped a zillion pics, shared weekend plans, and free-styled ghost stories. As always, the fun continued into the early morning and Katherine found that tonight, in particular, she was grateful for this perfectly joyful ending to her rollercoaster ride of a week.

CHAPTER SEVEN
THE IDEA
SATURDAY

Katherine woke to the sound of screaming.

She bolted upright from her sleeping bag. *What was wrong?* It was mostly dark out and the other girls still had their eyes closed, though it wasn't clear if they were asleep or just wishing they were. As her eyes began to focus and she processed where she was, Katherine realized it was just Naomi's baby brother, demanding to be picked up. A vague recollection of similar sounds played across her memory. *Thank God Mia had outgrown that!*

Flopping down into her puffy sleeping bag, Katherine tried desperately to go back to sleep, but sleep wouldn't come. Panic and embarrassment engulfed her, leaving muscles clenched and the air in her chest tight.

The audition!

She could have cried, remembering briefly the fun night they had just had a few hours earlier. Couldn't she just think about that? Why was *this* plaguing her now?!

Oh right.

It had been late in the evening when they'd gotten around to their mani-pedis and no one had had much energy for karaoke, so they found themselves instead lounging and listening to the instrumental tracks while waiting for their freshly manicured fingers and toes to dry. And as often happens when old friends come to a lull in conversation, they began to reminisce. Which was nice, until 'remember when' turned into 'I can't wait until'. Before long, talk of seventh grade was in full swing. Finally— junior high! True, they'd be the youngest kids in the school, but at least they'd be *around* older and cooler kids. And the teachers wouldn't treat them like babies—or worse, like *role models*.

Katherine kept quiet and tried her best to hide in plain sight, but it wasn't long before Bridget noticed, and gently reminded the others that they weren't all going to be at the same school. Her heart stopped. *Oh God. Is this really how the evening was going to go? Would she have to talk about the audition here and now?* She was having such a great time and that would just ruin everything.

But fate took pity on her when, at that very moment, Naomi's mom called down to say that everyone upstairs was going to bed now... perhaps it was time for the girls to do the same? Grudgingly, they made half-hearted attempts to bring the night to a close. And although they had no intention of actually going to sleep, bedtime routines kicked in. As toothbrushes and retainers were located and dibs taken on the bathroom, Katherine's crisis was averted. The conversation changed course and never did find its way back to the loaded topic that Katherine so desperately wanted to avoid. But it played on her mind as she drifted off and slept fitfully, dreaming of lost keys and missing pages.

***

Maren was always the first to leave. Saturday was a full-on dance day, so she was already dressed and ready to go before her friends had even considered changing out of their pajamas. Still, by 10am, Bridget and Katherine were rolling up their sleeping bags and collecting their stuff in a sleep-deprived haze. The fun of the previous night was drifting into memory and their bodies ached from a night on the hard floor. When Katherine's mom picked her up 30 minutes later, she had all but forgotten the fun and she found herself focusing squarely on the darkness. Last night's dream played on a loop in her mind's eye and the memory of the audition was blazing in a harsh stream of florescent light. *All of her plans and hopes destroyed.* Tears played at the edges of her eyes and threatened to overwhelm them. Turning toward the window, she squeezed them shut and willed the tears away. She would not cry. She did not want to remember. And she had zero interest in talking about it.

As they pulled into the driveway, Katherine opened the car door and quickly grabbed her things. She raced inside and up the stairs to her room. *A shower.* A shower would help, and it would keep her mom from checking in on her. Mrs. Keyes always knew when something was wrong, and Katherine could not face her right now. Not until the images were pushed firmly out of her mind and she could busy herself with other things.

Other things! Katherine thought with a start, as the shampoo ran down her face. She had totally forgotten about Charlotte. *What time was she coming again?* Hurriedly, she rinsed her hair, dried off, and wrapped herself in a fluffy purple robe. She checked her phone. 3pm. *OK, there was time.* What were those songs Charlotte had texted her yesterday? Their names weren't familiar, but maybe she knew them and just didn't know what they were called?

Nope. A quick internet unearthed two totally new songs. Listening to the tunes while she picked out a shirt and jeans, Katherine began to normalize. Some flippy sequins and ripped knees helped get her in the mood. As she sat at the keyboard with headphones on, two hours passed in a blur of experimentation, careful listening, and messing around with her synthesizer's sound effects. She was so caught up in her musical mind that she didn't even notice when her mom peeked in, watched for a minute or two, and then gently closed the door with a relieved smile in her eyes. Soon the songs were figured out and some notes written down in a multicolored sequin journal that, until now, had sat purposeless on her shelf. Katherine imagined it had been waiting for just this moment to come into use—her band journal.

And she still had an hour and a half before Charlotte arrived.

Katherine surveyed her cozy bedroom with new eyes. She loved her deep purple walls and colorful oversized paintings. But it was kind of small. There wouldn't be much room for her and Charlotte to move once the guitar and amp were set up. Flopping on a giant beanbag chair, she thought about her house and where else they could possibly practice that would give them more room to maneuver. The rec room was out—that was Declan's domain and she knew he'd be down there playing video games or working out. The piano room could work, but it was right next to the kitchen and right above the rec room, so the likelihood of being yelled at to turn down the volume was pretty high (she didn't really want to be near her piano right now anyhow). The TV room was clearly a no-go…

A thought struck her. *Could the garage work?* She'd heard about bands that practiced in their garage—they even called themselves 'garage bands'. And, unlike most of her friends' garages which were piled up with boxes and bikes and lawnmowers, hers was remarkably neat, so conceivably it could work. But did it even have plugs? *Was it warm enough?* Never thinking of that space as a *room* before, she needed to investigate.

Walking through the mental checklist she had made on the way to the garage, Katherine scrutinized its potential. There were plugs on all three walls, extension cords coiled up neatly on the wall, heaters (although it was already a pretty comfortable temperature), and a bunch of old purple and blue milk crates they could use as seats. She stood back and scanned the room with fresh eyes. It was built for two vehicles, and while it was used for storage, the shelving went right up against the walls—the rest of the space was reserved for cars that had never made it inside, which meant there was plenty of room to set up and play. The whole band could fit there, actually. And Dad kept it so clean, there wasn't much more than a sweep required, and maybe a few cobwebs to be vacuumed up. She shook her head in disbelief. *It was perfect!* Katherine felt a small tingle of excitement.

Grudgingly, Declan agreed to help her move the DX-7 back to the garage and, after setting it up on its stand, even her brother admitted it looked kind of cool. Sizing the room up, she felt a little color would be nice and looked behind the shelves for her stashes of stored artwork. There she found several oversized canvases she had almost forgotten. Bright and colorful, she propped three up around the room, covering a good chunk of the storage bins and adding significantly to the atmosphere. She sat on two milk crates to test their potential as seats and laid a colorful placemat over a spare bin to make a small table. Then, thirty minutes before Charlotte arrived, she stood back to take it all in, and felt that little tingle grow.

"This is *awesome!*" her bandmate gushed, before even saying hello. "Totally awesome! Oh my gosh, it's absolutely *perfect!*" Katherine smiled, proud of her afternoon's work. "These paintings are so cool—did you paint them? They look like your style… Milk crates—excellent—so much better than chairs! And *oh wow*—a DX-7? Classic synth!" As she soaked up the vibe, an idea sparked, like a lightbulb turning on in a dark room.

"Kat," she said, "we have to have the band here."

CHAPTER EIGHT
THE IMPROVISATION
SUNDAY

Sunday would be a day of rest—literally. Katherine's week had been nuts and she was exhausted. Between the audition and the rock band venture; the sleepover, garage redo, and accompanying gig, she felt like she'd just stepped off the world's longest, curviest roller coaster. She would sleep in, lounge in her pajamas, and spend the entire day in rest-and-recovery mode.

So much for best laid plans. Katherine woke at dawn—wide awake. But unlike her early rise yesterday, today she felt well rested and full of energy. The jam session had been so awesome, it left her wanting more. She couldn't wait until Tuesday to play again, so instead of rolling over and trying to get back to sleep, she quickly dressed and went downstairs, poured a big mug of tea, and made her way to the garage. It was a warm spring day and the sun shone through the narrow window on top of the garage door and under the crack at the bottom. Still buoyed up from her practice with Charlotte, the morning sun felt a little like the universe trying to make up for deserting her last week.

Katherine plugged in her headphones and put them on, and for the first time in almost a week, her well-formed habits kicked in. She started off with a flurry of scales and arpeggios (which she'd never done on the keyboard before), and it took just a moment to get used to the lighter weight of the keys. It felt good to get her fingers really moving again. Not yet ready to follow through with the rest of her piano routine (Step 1: Review the old stuff, Step 2: Practice the new stuff, Step 3: Polish the bits that were giving her trouble, Step 4: Finish up with the pieces she loved), she was able to brush off that impulse surprisingly quickly and instead jump into the songs she and Charlotte had worked on.

It felt *so good* to let loose and play. Technique-wise, she knew, these particular songs were a thousand times easier than what she normally played, but *music-wise* they spoke to a part of her soul that desperately needed *this* music at *this* time. Katherine played around with the songs and tried out some ideas, adding bits as she went, and before long found that she had wandered far away from where she had started and was instead improvising something new.

Improvising! The thought and the word hit her like a bolt of lightning. Katherine sat back and marveled at the dual facts that she a) could do that and b) didn't know she could do that. In fact, she'd always shied away from jazz band for that very reason. Maybe it was her imagination, but this not only *felt* good, it *sounded* good, too!

Pulling out her phone, she took a deep breath then pressed

record, laid the phone on the amp and started to play again. This version wasn't exactly the same as the one from a few minutes ago, but it was pretty close—similar enough to give her a sense as to whether or not she was totally out to lunch. With her breath held again, she pressed *play* and closed her eyes.

IT WAS GOOD!

She stopped the recording and opened her eyes. Not only was she, *Classical Kathy,* playing *rock* music in a *rock* band, she was now *improvising*… in her super cool 'tricked-out' (Charlotte's words) garage… and it sounded good!

In that surreal moment, Katherine again had a strange sensation of hovering above the room, looking down, as she tried in vain to reconcile the piano demon who had totally blown her audition less than a week ago with this new, creative, almost confident kid in her garage.

***

Addison's yell startled her out of her reverie, "She's down here!"

Addison turned back towards her sister, "What's going on, Kat?" she asked. "When did you come down here? Everyone's been looking for you!"

"Sorry…!" she said, in a confused haze, "what time is it?"

"10:30. But Mom's been having a heart attack for at least half an hour. She went to call you for Mass and couldn't find you anywhere. She's on high alert—I recommend an oversized apology."

Laying her headphones on the crate and turning off the

keyboard, Katherine made her way to the kitchen where she found a flustered Mom, sitting at the table, fighting to get a brush through Mia's hair.

"Hey, Mom…" she said in a hesitant voice. "Sorry to freak you out. I woke up early and went down to practice. But no one else was up, so I put my headphones on. I didn't want to wake you guys." She stopped for air as Mrs. Keyes paused the hair battle and looked up. Katherine continued, "I guess I got caught up in it—I didn't know you were looking for me."

"It's okay, Katherine. I never thought to look in the garage—I forgot that you'd set yourself up in there. I'll know better next time." She quicky changed gears, "We're going to church for 11:00, so hurry up and get ready."

***

The car ride to church involved the usual a) litany of complaints from Declan that he was old enough to decide for himself whether or not he wanted to go—and he didn't, so why were Mom and Dad forcing him? b) Mia singing the latest song from her favorite Youtuber on a loud and not entirely tuneful loop, and c) Addison telling them both to shut it and just be quiet for once. *What fun.*

Katherine didn't mind going to church. Sometimes she even liked it. Not that she was always paying attention… And today was one of those in-and-out of focus days—listening here and there, but mostly enjoying the quiet of the space to hear herself think. The week had had such lows—well, one low in particular—and such highs. It seemed like so much had happened since she was here last Sunday, silently practicing her pieces for her audition. *Pieces she hadn't actually touched in almost a week*, she remembered, realizing with a start that she had a piano lesson tomorrow.

She hadn't talked to Mrs. Bellamy since just after the audition. Her teacher had asked her to call as soon as she was done, which she did. But Katherine hadn't told her much—it went fine, the adjudicators were nice, aural skills were pretty good, the school was cool. *No details about what had happened.* And she really didn't look forward to reliving it with her tomorrow. If it were anyone else, she could probably get away with glossing over the story without details, but she knew that wouldn't work here. Mrs. Bellamy knew her well, and when they were face-to-face, she would see right through any attempt at deflection.

As if the looming piano lesson wasn't stressful enough, tomorrow would also be her first rehearsal with the choir, so Katherine resigned herself to spending the afternoon at the piano, learning the accompaniment. And, she discovered later, it was a good thing she did—*yikes*, what a lot of notes! It was all too clear why a more advanced pianist was needed. Truth be told, it wasn't even fair to call it a choir song with piano accompaniment— it was more like a piano piece with choir accompaniment. But *whatever*, lots of stuff wasn't fair.

The combination of two nights with not enough sleep and two stressful events coming up tomorrow had made Katherine slightly grumpy. She tried to remember that line from Mass about not worrying about tomorrow, but try as she might to push it aside, the worry was stuck in a tight little knot in the pit of her stomach and it refused to budge.

CHAPTER NINE
THE CHOIR
MONDAY

A night of tossing and turning, on top of the two shortened nights before, left Katherine feeling wrecked. The day she had been dreading was here and she was too tired to even think. Could she stay home 'sick' because she was too tired to go to school? Was that a thing? It should be, but she didn't think her mom would go for it. She downed a giant mug of tea, determined to ignore its annoyingly pert happy face emojis. While Katherine assumed the smiling yellow spheres represented how she was meant to feel when it was empty, in reality she was only marginally less wrecked and still not in a happy face space.

The texts started to ding as she dressed and got ready for the day. Her friends never could wait until lunch on Mondays to catch up, so the flurry of back-and-forth this morning was nothing new. The banter and its relentless dinging were simultaneously annoying and uplifting. And as Katherine got caught up in the chat, her sleepiness started to dissipate, and her anxieties began to recede. Bridget and Maren were a funny pair—they soon had her laughing out loud at their silent, silly chat, which persisted all the way through the ride to school. By the time Katherine arrived, she felt a million times better and was grateful, not for the first time, to have such awesome friends.

There was a sub for Math, which meant a free block to catch up on all the news. It didn't *actually* mean that, but that's definitely how the class interpreted it. Just what Monday morning called for! The before-school texting had already caught them up on the weekend's events, so the conversation now turned to the following, in random and returning order:

Bridget's latest crush

The possibility of a school talent show

Was there a test coming up in History?

Maren's braces coming off soon

The latest hair tools (as seen on *TikTok*)

How to create a perfectly sun-kissed look without actually getting suntanned (also from *TikTok*)

Bridget's latest crush

The current girlfriend of Bridget's latest crush

And finally, would there be school dance before the end of the year?

Exactly the kind of anything-but-music chat that Katherine needed.

By lunchtime, yesterday's worry knot had loosened to a mere hint of concern as she and Bridget made their way to choir together. Bridget was thrilled to have her join the group, if only for this one song. She couldn't wait to hear her friend play with them! Katherine was less excited, but not nearly as stressed as she had been each time she'd imagined this rehearsal over the course of the last week.

This was often the case, she found—that she stressed and fretted about performances, or anything resembling them, up until the actual day of, but then she felt mostly ok—at least until it got close to her turn. And *usually* (*last Monday was a clear exception*), everything went great, in spite of any butterfly action. She wished she could remember this in real time on the days and weeks of stress before each performance. Then, maybe, she would be less anxious. But somehow the memory didn't take. It sounded a little bit like the way she'd heard people talk about giving birth. Terrible and the most pain ever, but as soon as the baby arrived it was all forgotten. *Until the next time.*

The rehearsal room was huge. Its tiered floors, in a kind of semi-circle shape, meant that everyone could see the conductor without having to stand on risers. The choir was big, too. Katherine tried to count the singers, but they kept streaming in and taking their places between people she had already counted, so she lost track. It seemed like maybe 75 or more by the time the warm-ups had started. She hadn't realized how many kids she knew who were into singing. All kinds of kids, too—cool, uncool, smart, less smart, athletic, definitely-not-athletic, artistic, techie— representatives from pretty much the whole study body. And there was Charlotte! She caught her eye and smiled. Charlotte loved music so it made sense she'd be here, but somehow seeing her electric guitar-playing friend in choir surprised her at first. Even more surprising was the fact that her butterflies hadn't really kicked in. *Yet.* They were probably just watching and waiting.

Katherine Lost

***

Katherine found a seat in the back of the room by the windows and alternated her gaze between the scene in front of her and the nest of bright blue eggs in the tree outside. It really was remarkable how music could bring together people who wouldn't normally connect otherwise.

The choir was really good and the songs Mr. Bertulli had chosen were awesome. First, there was an upbeat showtune, with choreographed movements and everything. It was obviously something they'd been working on for quite a while—the singing and the movements were tight. Katherine found herself wistfully wishing she were part of it.

The next one was slower, with challenging harmonies and the choir split up into a lot of different parts. It was complicated and not as polished as the first one—which explained why so much more rehearsal time was spent working through its details.

If Katherine was being honest, the third song was kind of weird, and a little jarring at first. There were a lot of interesting sounds involved, but not sounds she'd consider musical. Closing her eyes, she tried to make sense of it, and in doing so discovered something unexpected—she liked it. In spite of herself, she found that the odd, but interesting combinations of sounds painted an awesome and awe-inspiring picture of spring! Turning her gaze back to the nest, the song now seemed to make total sense, working in perfect harmony with the scene outside the window.

The spring song and nature scene had the combined effect of momentarily calming and distracting Katherine from the reason she was there in the first place. So, when Mr. Bertulli introduced her song and invited Katherine to the piano, the butterflies that had been lying in wait were startled and began flittering around in her stomach. Choosing to think of them as part of the deal, she didn't even attempt to ignore them, but rather squared her focus on the tasks at hand. While the choristers rifled through their folders, Katherine adjusted the bench, took a few deep breaths, and sent a small glance skyward, in hopes that the heavens would smile on her at this particular moment, in front of all these people.

Giving more credit than she felt she deserved, Mr. Bertulli turned toward Katherine. "I just want to give you a heads up that you may need to go a little slower than you planned. We've only been working on this song for a short time and it's still a bit rough around the edges." He went on, "Keep an eye on me as best you can—we'll likely be stopping fairly frequently for now." To her great surprise, he went even further, "I want to thank you for taking this on. I know it's a tough piece and you've only had it for a minute. If you need to leave notes out or drop out at any point, that's just fine. We've got time to sort out the kinks. No one expects it to be perfect today."

Katherine felt like the world had tilted. Never had she ever played in front of this many people without understanding that it all had to be perfect. But then, she had never been at a rehearsal like this before. In spite of the fact that there were lots of people in the room and everyone except the teacher was facing her, they were all in this together. It wasn't actually a performance—it was *a rehearsal*. The thought echoed in her ears. But not for long, because Mr. Bertulli's hands were soon raised and the room hushed. He began to conduct, and before she knew it, she was playing the lengthy piano introduction in front of 75+ schoolmates. So focused was she on the score before her and the hands conducting in her peripheral view that she didn't give a thought to any of the usual distractions—people coughing, doors closing, candy wrappers crinkling. *She just played.* And then the choir joined in and the sound was glorious. Katherine felt she was part of something big and beautiful, larger than life. *And only a part of it*—not the one-person show that had always been her experience.

In a way, this rehearsal felt similar to her time with Charlotte's band. Without looking for it or expecting it, she seemed to have stumbled upon a new way of making music, and Katherine liked it. By the end of the rehearsal, she felt great—the butterflies settled quietly back in their resting places, and a mixture of calm and happiness flowed through her.

It felt like peace.

CHAPTER TEN
THE LESSON
MONDAY

The afternoon slipped by and before she knew it, Katherine found herself knocking on her piano teacher's door. Mrs. Bellamy lived in a beautiful old brownstone. She enjoyed telling guests that its original owner had been a beer magnate, who famously had trouble navigating both the steep stairs to the front door and the spiral staircase inside. Wonderfully ornate banisters and trim, and a polished oversized foyer made you feel like you'd entered the home of a fancy rich socialite—which was about the furthest possible description from her beloved piano teacher as you could imagine. Mrs. Bellamy was the epitome of humble and unassuming. She was kind and generous and didn't give a hoot about impressing people or doing things for show. Her standards were high, everyone knew, but she cared as much for her students' well-being as people as she did for their growth as musicians. It was kind of ironic that she lived in such a showy home when she herself was the picture of simplicity.

Katherine had dreaded this moment. For the last seven days, there wasn't one in which she hadn't tried to imagine telling Mrs. Bellamy the full story about her audition. Not that she expected her teacher to be angry or anything. She just knew that Mrs. Bellamy was aware of how important the audition was—and that she would be sad for her. Katherine didn't think she could cope with the complexities of making someone she loved sad on her behalf, especially while she was still coming to terms with her own grief. Still, she stood there with her heart quickening, waiting for her teacher to open the door and invite her in with the usual smile of delight. Mrs. Bellamy loved her students— they all knew it. And they wanted so much to be successful—for their own sake, yes, but also to make her proud.

It took a moment longer than usual, but, as expected, Mrs. Bellamy's face lit up when she saw Katherine on the stoop. She wore an apron and an oven mitt, and the house smelled like lemons.

"Katherine! Come on in. I was just making lemon loaves. Michael is coming this weekend and he's made his usual request. You know my family is crazy about anything lemon!" She closed the door and wiped her hands in her apron. "Paul is home sick today, so I thought I'd use the extra time before your lesson to get a head start on the baking. Are you hungry? Why don't we sample them to see if they're fit to eat, and you can tell me all about your audition!"

Katherine's heart sank. She loved lemon loaf, but the knot that had been growing in her stomach was now full sized and it left no room for anything else. Still, she followed her teacher into the house and laid her books in the music room while Mrs. Bellamy put the kettle to boil in the kitchen. When they both had steaming mugs in front of them and a plate of lemon loaf between them, she eagerly prompted, "So, tell me all about it!"

Katherine told her everything, except the detail she'd been avoiding. She knew the conversation would get there, but she needed time to work up to it. "The school was amazing. All the classrooms were set up for music. There were pianos everywhere, and drum sets, and audio systems." Her deep brown eyes sparkled as she pictured it all. "There were no normal classrooms that I could see—they all seemed prepared for rehearsing. And there were no normal desks, either, only those chairs with the little desk arms that move up and down. The classrooms and the hallways were full of artwork, which was awesome. It really made it feel like a creative place." Katherine felt a sudden desperate desire to study there, as a pang of longing ran through her. She pushed it away brusquely and continued. "The tests were okay. I mean, it was a pretty intense environment, and the kids looked totally stressed, but I think I did pretty well in them all—even sight reading, if you can believe it."

Smiling sheepishly, she paused. She had run out of things to talk about other than the main event. And she just didn't know how to begin.

"How did your pieces go?" Mrs. Bellamy made the segue for her. She was not one for beating around the bush, and Katherine knew from experience that she could spot avoidance tactics from a mile away. "How did you play?" she added gently.

With the vague sense that she knew exactly the train-wreck it had been, but was too polite to say, Katherine held her mug with both hands and looked deep into its depths, her heart racing. "Well… um… Well, it could have been better." She took a long, deep breath and exhaled slowly. "To be honest, I think I kind of blew it."

Mrs. Bellamy looked at her quietly for a moment, her blue eyes kind. "Start at the beginning, Katherine. Walk me through it, okay?"

"Okay." She took another deep breath. This was it. There was no turning back now, and no more pretending it didn't happen. Bizarrely, she felt somewhat better, after this long week, to be on the cusp of sharing her burden with *someone.*

"They asked for the Bach first. I took it a bit faster than usual —I was nervous, I guess, and I just started without setting the tempo. It went okay, though—I was able to manage it without falling apart, but it definitely got my heart racing."

"Well, that one can absolutely be faster, Katherine—I wouldn't be concerned about that. The only reason to go a little slower, like we planned, is to keep your fingers from getting tangled up. If they didn't, then that's great! What did you play next?"

"Schumann. That one was fine. I don't remember any big problems with it. Actually, it sounded really good in the big empty concert hall. Although being up on stage with only five people in the audience was pretty intimidating. Especially since I knew they were all judges."

"I know—auditions are strange like that. You have the smallest audience, but also one of the most potent, right? I often think of adjudicators as gatekeepers, deciding who can enter and who can't, and that's…" She stopped abruptly mid-sentence.

"But you know, Katherine—all of these judges, they have been in your shoes many times, and they've also seen so many students in exactly the same hotseat you were in. They're more understanding than you might think."

They both sipped their tea for a quiet moment before she asked, "Did you play the Mozart?"

The words she had been dreading hung in the air, as Katherine tried and failed to think of the right words to explain.

Deep breath, Katherine.

Hesitantly, she began, "I played the Mozart." She paused. "It started off well…" Another deep breath. "And most of it went pretty well, I think." She'd forgotten about that… Katherine's chest felt tight as she reflected on what happened next. "But as I got close to the end, I started to think about how well it was all going, and that it was almost over, and how much I wanted to go to the school…" Her gaze and her voice were far away. "And then I suddenly realized that I had totally lost my place. I didn't know what my next notes were—I just blanked…" Tears filled her eyes and pooled at the corners, threatening to trickle down if she so much as blinked.

Mrs. Bellamy retrieved a box of tissues from the counter and waited a moment before nudging her on. "What did you do?" she asked.

Katherine willed back the tears, biting the corner of her lip as she sucked in the air slowly. "The only thing I could think of—I jumped to one of the starting places we'd practiced, and then just powered through to the end. I left out that whole section." Staring at her hands, clenched and motionless in her lap, Katherine shook her head as if to erase the memory. "It was awful."

"Did you stop for long?"

"I don't know. It's hard to say. I think it was just for a moment. As soon as I realized the notes weren't going to come, I jumped ahead. I kind of panicked, I guess."

"And then what about the Debussy? Did you play it?"

"I did. It was fine. I mean, I was so rattled by the Mozart that I'm not really sure how it went, to be honest. I didn't have any big mess-ups or anything, but I have no idea how it sounded."

Mrs. Bellamy's eyes twinkled as she put her hand on Katherine's and looked deep into her sad eyes. "Katherine," she said with a light in her voice, "I'm *so* proud of you!"

Stunned, Katherine reached for a tissue.

"It sounds like the audition went beautifully!"

Maybe she hadn't been clear in her description of the event. Mrs. Bellamy was kind, but not someone who'd deny bad news when she heard it.

Katherine looked up at her, dumbfounded. "I had a massive memory slip! It was a complete disaster!"

Mrs. Bellamy's sympathetic eyes continued to look straight into hers and she spoke in a firm voice. "What I just heard was not a disaster. Far from it! Katherine, I've been an adjudicator. And although some judges can be tough, I can tell you that most would see things my way, which is like this: You played four diverse and difficult pieces very well. You successfully managed a fast tempo in a complicated piece. You played beautifully and musically (I know this because you don't know any other way to play)." She smiled, "And you navigated a memory lapse like a pro! I couldn't be prouder if you had told me that it was all 100% perfect."

Katherine was floored. This conversation had strayed far

from her expectations. *Was it possible that she had played well and not realized it? Was she so caught up in the need to be perfect that she forgot that anything else mattered?*

"So, you don't think they noticed the mistake in the Mozart?" she asked, hopefully.

"Oh, I'm sure they wouldn't have missed it. Mozart is terribly transparent," Mrs. Bellamy burst that bubble of hope. "But I'd be willing to bet they were as impressed by your ability to keep going as they were by your beautiful playing."

"I thought I had totally bombed." Katherine wiped the tears from her eyes with the back of her hand, forgetting all about the Kleenex box in front of her. "You honestly don't think I did?" she pleaded.

"No, I definitely don't think you did. In fact, it sounds like you did remarkably well. That was a stressful situation and you handled it with grace." She stood up and gave Katherine a big hug. "You should feel very proud, Katherine," she said. "I am."

Katherine choked back her overwhelmed emotions. It felt as though a tidal wave was crashing over her. She knew her face must be red and splotchy, but she refused to let her feelings overtake her. Quickly, she changed the topic.

"Mr. Bertulli asked me to accompany the choir."

"Yes, I know. Mrs. Gibbons called me to ask if I thought you could handle that piece, and I told her you'd be perfect for it. It's time for you to start playing with other musicians. You're young, but you've got the chops, Katherine—you can handle it. Bach and Mozart are amazing, and its lovely to have practice time on your own, but it can get lonely for pianists if they only ever play by themselves." She added, "Have you played with them yet?"

Katherine nodded, "Today."

"And...?"

"And it was great—I really enjoyed it." Katherine replied.

"Wonderful! I'm so glad." Laying the mugs and plates in the sink, she led the way to the piano room. "Would you like to start with that choir piece today? I'd love to hear it."

And so, as they moved into the familiar lesson routine, Katherine sensed a weight had been lifted from her shoulders. In its place was an odd mix of feelings – relief, exhaustion, and for the first time in a week, the teensiest bit of hope.

CHAPTER ELEVEN
THE CONVERSATION
TUESDAY

C an we jam at your place?"

Tuesday's session was going well. The band now had four songs, in various stages of readiness, but they needed rehearsal time outside of school if they were really going to gel. Two lunch periods just weren't enough for any serious progress—by the time they made it to the room, set everything up, ate lunch, and saved time at the end to put everything away again, there was only a small window left to actually practice. If they were really going to do this, they needed more time to work out new ideas and refine their sound.

"Kat has this awesome set-up in her garage—just, like, a really cool vibe," Charlotte raved. "We could be, like, an actual 'garage band'!" Charlotte's eyes sparkled at the prospect. "What do you think, Kat? Can it be our jam space?"

All eyes were on her. This whole band thing was moving fast. Jumping into new things wasn't usually Katherine's way—she liked to ease in slowly and make sure it was for her before fully committing. But for some reason, she didn't feel the need to slow things down this time. Playing with the band felt right and, like the others, she wanted more, not less of it. Plus, she was happy that Charlotte thought her garage was cool. "Yeah—okay. Sure!" she said. "I mean, I'll need to check with Mom and Dad, since I did kind of commandeer the space… but I think they'll be okay with it."

The four bandmates got out their phones to share contact information, making a tentative plan for Saturday.

***

After school, Katherine met up with Naomi, Maren, and Bridget. She hadn't seen the girls since Saturday morning, and in spite of a significant amount of texting and *Instagram* updates, there was some catching up to do. Bridget was on Student Council and she had breaking news to share—there was definitely going to be a talent show!

"They're still finalizing the date, but I think it will be pretty soon—maybe in a couple of weeks. We still have to decide if it should be during the day or at night. I mean, during the day we'd get to miss classes, so that's a definite plus, but night just has a different feel, you know? More… *special*. We're meeting again tomorrow. Mrs. Weldon gets to make the final decision, but she usually listens to the committee. I like that about her. Anyhow, she said she wanted to make a decision this week."

"Is it for everyone and, like, any kind of talent?" Maren asked.

"Yes, and I think so. I'm sure you can do a dance. You must have a million to choose from." Maren had been competing all spring, they knew, although she rarely talked about it. She had a zillion costumes and probably as many routines. The girls knew that a school talent show would be small potatoes compared to the performances she normally gives, but they each silently assumed she would sign up.

"I don't think we've had a show since fourth grade, have we?" Katherine reflected.

Bridget shook her head, "No—and I've been dying to try out my material." Bridget was the funniest person Katherine knew, a natural comedian. She'd been trying her ideas out on her friends for as long as anyone could remember, but only casually. Not in a formal show with an audience and everything. The excitement in Bridget's voice was infectious.

"Do you have to try out?" Katherine asked, with a flutter of butterfly activity in her stomach. "And do you want to run your routine by us?"

"I think so—auditions, I mean. I don't have all the details, but I'll let you know as soon as I do. And yes, I would love to run my routine for you guys! Not yet, though. I need to practice and get it a tight first. Maybe on the weekend?"

Katherine realized she hadn't told her friends about her new band. "Yeah—for sure. I can't do Saturday morning, but I'm pretty open otherwise." She paused for a moment before shyly adding, "I, uh… I started playing in this band and we're practicing on Saturday morning."

"Is it that band that Mrs. Gibbons asked you to join? The kids-and-seniors one?"

"No, not that one. I mean, I did join it, but we finished up for the season a few weeks ago." Though she couldn't put her finger on why, Katherine realized she was a little nervous to tell them. "Um—it's actually a rock band," she heard herself say, with her voice rising at the end as if it were a question. "It's just me and a few girls from school. They needed a keyboard player and asked me to help out. It's only since last week, so I've literally played with them twice. But we planned to meet up on Saturday morning…" she blurted out in a stream of information. Katherine's gaze was squarely on the sidewalk as she spoke. This was so weird. She was nervous to see her friends' reaction.

She looked up slowly to see surprised, happy faces.

"That's amazing, Katherine! I guess we'll have to call you 'Kat' more often now, though, if you're going to be a rock star. I'm so excited for you! Can we come hear you?" Bridget exclaimed.

"What songs are you doing?" Naomi asked. "And do you have a teacher, or is it just you guys?"

Katherine answered their questions and filled them in on the details. And she felt so elated and relieved by their response that she just wanted to hug them. Instead, she blurted out, "Do you want to have a sleepover at my place on Saturday and I can tell you all about it?

***

"Mom…?" Katherine asked, poking her head into mom's study when she got home. "Would it be okay if my band practices here on Saturday morning? The garage is already set up, and if no one needs it maybe I can keep it this way…?" And then, in her excitement to just get everything finalized, she added the second request. "And also—can Bridget and the gang sleep over on Saturday night?"

Mrs. Keyes looked up from her laptop as if still deep in thought and pushed her reading glasses up on her head. She paused for a moment with that look she got when she was in the middle of something and had to quickly shift gears.

"Oh—sorry to interrupt… I can ask you later." Katherine moved to close the door.

"No, no that's fine," her mom said. "I was just about to finish up here. I'm grading—my least favorite part of my job." Her mom loved to teach, but she hated grading papers. *Why does everything have to be 'worth something'?* she'd often complain. *Isn't learning value enough?*

Closing the computer, she patted the spot next to her on the compact couch. "Come sit down." She began to process Katherine's requests. "Saturday… Yeah, I think that would be okay," she said after a moment of mentally reviewing the entire family's calendar. "And I don't see why you shouldn't keep using the garage," she added. "We don't really use it for anything other than storage, so if you want to get some mileage out of the space, I think that's great."

Katherine smiled. "Awesome! Thanks mom."

"I like what you did with it, by the way. It's like a kind of funky artist's studio." Katherine smiled. That's exactly what she was going for.

"Tell me about your band," her mom said. "Charlotte seems

nice. Who else is in it? And how long have you been playing together? You've kept this one under your hat!"

"It's really new," Katherine said. "I started playing with them last week," she added. "It wasn't planned or anything— it just kind of happened. The other girls were already together. They were practicing in the band room and I was there when they were down a keyboard player, so I gave it a try." She paused for a moment, recalling the event. "I mean, I was a little nervous at first 'cause, well, I didn't really know how to play that kind of music… but it was really cool. And it wasn't all that hard— definitely not as hard as I thought it would be. I just needed to change up how I learn the songs—you know, 'cause there's no sheet music. I had to kind of listen and figure things out."

Mrs. Keyes smiled one of her proud, happy smiles. Katherine loved those. "You know, Katherine, I always wanted to be in a band… I would have loved that." She looked wistfully at Katherine, whose questioning expression begged for more. "I wanted to be a singer, and not just in my choirs…" She paused, deep in thought. "But I think I was just too scared about breaking out of my comfort zone and maybe not being any good at it, or about what people would think. I don't know." She drifted off. "But I sure am proud of you, Katherine." Looking directly at her daughter, she smiled. "You are such a brave girl. First, you audition for this fancy performing arts school—which, let's face it, was pretty daunting. And now you're branching out into a whole new type of music with a new group of friends." She paused for a moment, her eyes crinkling at the corners. "I think *you* are amazing."

Katherine didn't know what to say. On the audition day, her

mom had acted like the whole thing was totally normal, nothing to worry about. But she had thought it was intense, too! And these youthful dreams! Katherine had no idea—this was the first she heard of them. Seems like mom kept a few things under her hat, too. It was crazy how much you could learn about someone in just a few short minutes. But she had no idea how to respond. *Why were these ridiculous tears prickling at her eyes?!*

Moments later, still unable to find words, she opted instead for the only real communication that fit this particular moment. Leaning over, she wrapped her arms around her mom. And they stayed there, wrapped in the bond only a mother and daughter could know, until any need for words was gone.

CHAPTER TWELVE
THE ANNOUNCEMENT
WEDNESDAY

The willow was now in full bloom, no longer tragic, but rather, serene, its limbs swaying in the breeze. Katherine was entranced by their rhythmic flow—a much better use of her time, she felt, than listening to Mr. Ryan take attendance while the morning announcements played over the P.A. system. *Chess club after school tomorrow, reminder about cell phone policy, meeting for spring break building project…* The disembodied voice of Mrs. Weldon droned on and on. Sometimes Katherine wished they would just text or email the info, even if she rarely checked her account. She'd rather scan her messages once a day than have to suffer this monotony. Today, though, she was happy for the chance to gaze at the willow, and so was grateful for the background noise.

As she settled in to absorb up the tranquility of the moment, one announcement broke through and startled her out of her reverie. Its funny how your brain can tune things out while simultaneously monitoring for important words. Katherine perked up. *School-wide Talent Show. Next Friday. 7pm. Auditions Monday and Tuesday after school. Sign up outside the auditorium today.*

Her heart stopped for a moment and a flicker of electricity shot through her—excitement tinged with anxiety. Instinctively, Katherine reached for her phone, but was stopped by the watchful eye of Mr. Ryan. Thirty seconds after a P.A. lecture about cell phones in school was apparently the wrong time to text her bandmate. Hastily, she returned the phone to her bag, and to her great relief Mr. Ryan did not confiscate it. Flashing lights reflecting on the floor under her desk told her that not all of her friends were similarly constrained.

An eternity later, the bell rang. Covertly grabbing her phone and shoving it in her pocket, Katherine raced out of her teacher's view, then quickly scanned her messages. Charlotte was signing them up. *Does Tuesday work for everyone? Think about which song to play. Meet at band room lunchtime. SO EXCITED!!!*

***

The girls raced to the band room and, a quick set-up later, were ready to rehearse. So much excitement surrounded the show, but there was no time to chat yet—they needed to run their songs first as a reminder of what they were working with. All four were possibilities, though two were still pretty new to Aaliyah and Mariana.

"Silent vote?" suggested Charlotte. They each tore off a small piece of paper, wrote down their choice, and dropped it into an empty storage container they found by the filing cabinets. Mariana gave it a shake, then emptied the contents onto a desk. Two titles, with two votes each.

"Do you think we can perform them both?" Aaliyah voiced the question they were all thinking.

"I doubt it," Bridget responded. I think the time limit is pretty tight—four minutes, maybe? We'd only have time for one."

"Well, I guess we've narrowed it down, anyway," Katherine offered. "Should we play those two again?"

After two more rounds on the two options, they voted again. This time a unanimous winner emerged—a catchy tune with cool parts for everyone to play. And it was in good shape already. With some additional work, it would definitely be performance-ready.

As they packed up to head back to class, the girls solidified their plans. "Saturday, 10:00am at Katherine's house," Charlotte reminded. "Does anyone need to leave at a certain time?"

No one had any plans, or at least none that couldn't be changed. They all agreed this rehearsal was more important than anything else they had going on anyhow. They could meet at 10:00 and go as long as they needed.

"Just come over as soon as you're up. I'll open up the garage door and you can bring your gear straight in," said Katherine. "We can eat at my house. Mom loves to bake, so our rehearsal will give her a good excuse. And we can order pizza or something for lunch, if you want."

The bell rang, and they went back to class—with stars in their eyes and butterflies in their stomachs.

***

Maren, Naomi, and Bridget waited for Katherine on the school steps, excitedly discussing the talent show. Bridget had spent the previous evening refining her material. Four minutes, they had learned, was indeed the time limit. It wasn't much, but for a stand-up routine it was plenty. Only Bridget's was still at six and a half. She had to tighten it up. Could they help her narrow it down?

Maren was planning to do a tap routine she'd already performed at a few competitions. Clearly it was pretty tight already. "How many trophies for this one?" her friends inquired, in all seriousness.

Maren blushed, looking at her feet and mumbling, "Um, I don't know."

Not wanting to embarrass her further, they didn't press, but her friends knew that she rarely left the stage without one. Maren had spent every spring weekend for as long as Katherine could remember competing all around the state, and sometimes the country. They'd seen her dance many times over the years. Those legs and arms and face and costumes—well, the whole show-business package—was pretty impressive. Katherine wondered why she hadn't auditioned for *Valley View*, too.

Naomi had signed up for stage crew. Super organized and a master trouble-shooter, it was right up her alley. With no interest in being in the spotlight, she loved helping to bring it all together smoothly and seamlessly. Having worked crew on every single school play and musical, she was excited that this time her best friends would be in the show.

Since no one had any afterschool commitments, they went for ice-cream and continued the conversation until almost dinnertime. Katherine found herself thinking more and more about Maren and her dancing. It was clearly such an important part of her life—she was at the dance studio almost as much as she was at school. It was a miracle that she wasn't there right now, really, but it turned out that Wednesday was her late day at the studio—she didn't go until after dinner. *Why hadn't she auditioned with her?* she found herself wondering. *Valley View* had a great dance program. She wanted to ask, but she knew that would only lead to questions about her own audition, and she still didn't want to go there, even with her best friends. But it played on her mind.

So did the audition—the last one, and the next.

Oh no.

She had been so excited about playing with her band that she hadn't really processed what that meant—another audition. Her breath caught in her throat and suddenly she didn't think she could do it. But she couldn't pull out now—the band was counting on her. How was she going to get through this?

"What about you, Kat?" Bridget's voice cut through her thoughts.

"Huh?" She had no idea what they were talking about.

"Before you perform? What do you do to get you ready?"

"What do you mean? Sorry—I zoned out for a minute."

"We were talking about nerves, and Maren was telling us about this visualization thing she does before she goes onstage. Do you do anything like that?"

Katherine still didn't fully understand what they were talking about. "Uh, no. I don't think so. What do you mean by 'visualization'?"

"I just kind of close my eyes and picture the performance, imagining I'm backstage waiting for my turn, and going through the whole thing in my mind, you know, step by step: my dance being announced, getting into position, feeling the music, dancing, hearing the applause. And I just kind of focus on that and put other thoughts out of my mind." She shrugged, "My teacher taught me to do it a couple of years ago when I was really stressed about a tough competition. It seemed so weird at first, but I find it really helps."

"Cool," Katherine replied, silently reflecting on her own pre-performance process. *I sit frozen in my chair with my heart pounding, wipe my cold damp hands in my lap, ignore the need to go pee one more time, and try not to get too freaked out by how the kids before me are doing.* She didn't think this was the kind of thing her friends were asking about though, so she simply said, "I don't really do anything special." Then added politely, "But this sounds really interesting."

She noticed Maren looking at her with a curious gaze and she wondered what was up. But her phone blinked, summoning her home for dinner, so there was no time to ask.

CHAPTER THIRTEEN
THE CREATIVE FRENZY
THURSDAY AND FRIDAY

Two days seemed like an eternity to wait before the next band practice. Katherine could almost hear her mother's voice saying to treasure each day like a gift. And while she agreed that this this might be a good philosophy in general, she couldn't help thinking that some days were simply *better* gifts than others. Like, Thursday was maybe a donut shop gift card, but Saturday would be a full-on shopping spree. With less than a week to go, Katherine's instinct to practice incessantly was thwarted by the fact that her band couldn't meet until Saturday. Still, her thoughts rarely strayed from the band and the show. *And the audition.*

Almost two weeks later, the thought of an audition still caused her grief. It was a *totally* different kind of audition, she told herself. The keyboard part was way easier than any of her usual piano music. And she wouldn't be alone. She could probably forget the whole thing and the band would just keep going. Sure, the sound would be a little less full, but it would continue—and if she faked it by pretending to play, it was possible that no one would even notice. These points were a comfort when she stopped to rationalize the situation. The problem was, she didn't usually stop to think it all through, she just *felt*. And what she felt when she imagined herself back onstage wasn't great.

Pushing those feelings to the very bottom of her stomach, she balled them up tightly in the hope that they would stay there and leave the rest of her alone. Then she went about the business of practicing on her own and waiting. Looking forward to her friends coming over on Saturday and fearing the reason why.

***

With no rehearsals of any kind, Katherine found, for the first time in forever, that she had time to spare after school. This close to the end of the year there was minimal homework—and she was pretty good at cramming what she did get into the last minutes of class and lunchtime anyhow. Like her mom with grading, there wasn't much Katherine hated more than spending the time she wasn't at school on schoolwork. Avoiding it at all costs, she figured that what she lost by stuffing it into the school day was more than made up by not having to think about it once she got home.

Puttering around the house, unsure what to do, Katherine found herself drawn to the garage, thinking how strange it was that this would-be carpark had become her refuge. It was weird to think of it in those terms, she knew, but that's more-or-less how she saw it. So different from her cozy bedroom and her formal piano room—her mom nailed it when she said it was like an artist's studio. That's how Katherine had envisioned it, too—a blank canvas on which she could create and try new things without judgements or expectations.

In her heart, she knew she should go and practice her piano music. If she was being honest, the reason she had spare time right now was because she'd normally be at the piano. In her mind, she admitted that she had been delinquent lately, but still… she just didn't have it in her. Maybe she needed some new music or something, but at the moment she didn't feel like it. And she needed to honor those feelings, at least for a little while longer.

Katherine turned out the lights and closed the door that joined the house to the garage. She was restless. Without music filling her hours, she was at a loss as to what to do. While the kettle boiled and she raided the cookie jar, the blank canvas metaphor played in her mind, niggling and nudging as if there was something she needed to remember—or something she needed to do… The idea sparked and grew as she poured the steaming water into her giant happy face mug. And Katherine had the sense that maybe this time the smiling yellow orbs would get it right.

***

It had been a while since Katherine had spent any real time with her art, beyond what she did at school. Getting ready for the *Valley View* audition had taken up all of her time and energy for months beforehand, so painting had taken a back seat. But now that she was taking a breather, the creative itch came rushing back. And she had the perfect outlet for it.

With her parents on board, Katherine rummaged through her dad's paint supplies, all meticulously kept in labelled bins near the front of the garage. Finding a large, unused can of white acrylic paint, she pulled it out, along with some drop cloths, a rolling pan, a paint roller, and a brush. It took a while to move everything out from the walls and cover the bins with drop cloths, but once she had, the full breadth of her canvas was on display. Katherine's creative soul was bursting with excitement as she prepped the materials to lay a foundation for her work.

On Thursday night she fell into bed late, exhausted and exhilarated by the project before her, and fell asleep dreaming of swirls of color and abstract designs. On Friday evening, she made them a reality. With a focused eye and a flurry of ideas, Katherine played with reds and purples, blues and yellows so that they soon covered the walls all around, melding together to create a space that was uniquely hers.

When she finally felt it was finished, she laid down her brush and released the breath she had been holding for two days. Standing back to survey her masterpiece, Katherine's heart was happy.

CHAPTER FOURTEEN
THE GARAGE BAND
SATURDAY

It was a sunny Saturday morning when, at 9am, Katherine hoisted the garage door wide open. There was plenty of time, but she was eager to see her artwork in the light of day. Thrilled that she loved it as much today as she had last night, Katherine couldn't wait for her friends to get there. However, she was less thrilled about the strong paint smell that permeated the room and hoped that leaving the door open would clear the air before the band arrived.

Sure enough, by the time Mariana pulled up 45 minutes later, the paint scent was gone, and, in its place, the intoxicating aroma of cinnamon, sugar, and butter filled the air. *Cinnamon buns.* Katherine breathed it in deeply and smiled. In another life, she imagined, her mom must have been a baker and not an English professor. She sometimes wondered if she had missed her calling.

Hmmm, she thought, seemingly randomly, and yet with a

direct line of connection to the cinnamon buns—*better bring some baby wipes, too.*

Mariana, her dad, and Katherine worked swiftly to unload the drums and cymbals and stands and bring them into the garage. A quick goodbye later, Mariana turned to Katherine, "Oh my gosh, this is so amazing! I love this space. And what is that smell? I am so excited about the show! Where should I set up?"

Katherine figured she *must* be excited, since that was the most she had ever heard her friend say. Working side by side they put the set together, with Mariana guiding the process. Bass drum, toms, ride, crash, snare—Katherine's vocabulary was increasing by the second. And what was this? A cowbell?

"It's new," said Mariana. "I just got it yesterday. I'm in love with it—the sound is so freaking cool! I still have to figure out how to work it into the songs we're doing—or maybe I'll wait for different songs. But I still want to set it up with my gear. Want to hear it?"

Mariana played a few catchy rhythms on the cowbell and Katherine had to admit it was pretty cool. She wasn't convinced yet about how it would fit into the songs they'd been working on, but she was open. And besides, Mariana was the drummer, and it was kind of her call—or mostly her call, anyway—so she should have her moment to try it out.

They had just finished putting the set together when Aaliyah and Charlotte arrived. Like Mariana, they *oohed* and *aahed* over everything, then quickly got their instruments out—plugged in, tuned, warmed up—and dove straight into the song they had chosen for the show. Everything else would just have to be on hold until this one was polished. They ran it four times in a row without stopping, to kick start the rehearsal and see what needed to be done. When they paused briefly to assess things, Katherine's mom peeked in, smiling. In her hands was a tray of giant, gooey, cinnamon buns.

"Hi everyone!" she said cheerfully. "It sounds great in here!" Laying the tray on an upside-down milk crate, she added, "You've certainly livened up my morning!" Surveying the transformed garage with its vivid designs, she nodded at her daughter. "Katherine—you've outdone yourself."

***

"The walls look amazing, Kat," Charlotte said, as she tucked into the cinnamony deliciousness. "You're so lucky that your parents let you express yourself like this. I don't think I'd be allowed to use the walls in my house as a canvas." Mariana and Aaliyah nodded. "Me, either," said Aaliyah, "but then, I'm not an artist like you. This is really cool."

Katherine thought for a moment about her parents. They really did give her a lot of creative freedom… She made a mental note to thank them.

They savored the buns quietly for a few minutes before Mariana asked, between bites, "What do you think we should wear? Like, should we try to coordinate or something?"

The girls paused to think, "I mean, we could." Charlotte replied. "I never thought about it, but we *could* do something that kind of ties us together."

"Ok…" added Mariana, somewhat hesitantly, "as long as it's not too cutesy or anything. And not, like, everyone wearing exactly the same thing."

They all thought for a moment before jumping in again.

"We could just all wear jeans and different colored t-shirts—like, one red and one purple, and so on," offered Katherine.

"Or we could all wear black shirts, but, like, some of them long sleeved and some tank tops and some short sleeved." Charlotte added. They tried to picture themselves onstage.

Then Aaliyah, looking around the brightly colored room, offered an idea. "What if we had a bunch of colors, but all mixed up? We could tie dye our shirts—then they'd all be unique but still, like, connected."

"Oh my gosh, I love it!" exclaimed Mariana.

"Awesome!" echoed Charlotte and Katherine, at almost exactly the same time.

A plan quickly hatched. If they were going to wear the shirts to Tuesday's audition, they'd have to make them tomorrow. And, they figured, if they were getting together to color shirts, they might as well rehearse again, too. After a quick check-in with Katherine's parents to okay the gathering, they decided to leave the gear in place when they were finished later today and just pick things back up tomorrow, no set-up required.

The rest of the morning passed quickly but productively. Once they were satisfied that all the instrumental parts were clean and tight, the band began to play with musical components. They focused on tempo, dynamics, and especially balance. Mrs. Bellamy had taught Katherine how important balance is in keeping things interesting. She wondered briefly what her teacher would think of this application of her lesson. Of course, in piano the different musical lines are all played on the same instrument, so it's a matter of shifting the weight in your hands, but in a rock band, decisions need to be made about which player has something interesting happening in their part—they're the ones who are highlighted.

The whole process of listening to each section of the piece with a focus on what each instrument was doing was eye opening. By the time they worked through to the end, they all had a much better sense of the whole song, and not just their own part. When they ran it again, the difference this made was evident.

The band broke for lunch at around noon. While the original plan had been pizza, the warm spring day found them instead enjoying burgers in the backyard. It seemed like forever since Katherine had spent any time just hanging out and relaxing—she usually preferred to be busy—but the morning's work had been satisfying and she was enjoying the camaraderie with her bandmates as they sat on the swings and playhouse of the jungle gym. Her world was shifting and, unexpectedly, she was happy with where it seemed to be going.

***

Vocals were on the afternoon's agenda. With a band full of instrumentalists and no one designated exclusively as the singer, they'd agreed early on that everyone would contribute. Charlotte was the most confident singer, so she was the de facto lead on this song. The others sang back-up, though they soon figured out that singing harmony while also playing an instrument is not an easy thing to do. It took the better part of the afternoon to really figure it all out and get the vocal parts to gel, both with and without the instruments. The challenging, but rewarding, work made Katherine think, not for the first time, that the skills of rock musicians are highly underestimated.

It was late in the afternoon when they played it through for the last time, a much tighter and more professional version than where they had started that morning. And in the silence that lingered after the final chord was played, Katherine, once again, she had a weird sensation of looking down at her life from above, marveling at the notion of herself *playing and singing* in a *rock band*. Yes, the world had definitely shifted.

CHAPTER FIFTEEN
THE SLEEPOVER: TAKE 2
SATURDAY

When Maren, Bridget, and Naomi arrived at 5pm, they were surprised to find Katherine swinging in the yard. She was not known for her relaxed approach to life. In fact, it usually took her a while to loosen up whenever they got together. But today, it seemed, was different.

The band had rehearsed until almost 4pm, and when her bandmates were all picked up, Katherine found herself drawn back to the jungle gym, happy after a good day's work.

The girls climbed on—Maren on the second swing, Naomi on the climbing wall, and Bridget checking out the slide. It had been a while since any of them had even gone near a play structure—they were *too old* for that now. But they fell into it naturally, chatting and laughing all the while. Katherine told her friends all about her band, the songs they were playing, and their plans for a kind of 'look'.

Summer was definitely near; they could feel it. With only six weeks of school left, it felt like the weight was lifting with each degree higher the temperature crept and each minute later the sun shone in the evening sky. The girls stayed in the yard a long time, enjoying the evening air and each other's company. Then they made their way inside, stopping first at the garage to see where all the action had been taking place. And between admiring the artwork and checking out the band set-up, it didn't take long to decide that the slumber party should be there. With its unique and funky vibe, it was the perfect place to practice for the show.

***

As sleeping bags were unrolled, Katherine set up a couple of lamps she'd spotted in storage bins and tracked down some incandescent bulbs to add a nice glow. The overhead florescents were just too harsh for a Friday night. The usual activities kicked things off—the girls had a routine—and it was well into the evening before they turned their attention back to the show.

"Okay, I'm ready," Bridget said to her friends, abruptly changing gears after a lengthy karaoke session. "Pretend you're my audience and you don't know me and haven't heard my stuff before, okay? Can someone set a timer?"

As her friends turned to face her and Naomi opened the timer on her phone, Bridget closed her eyes for a moment and took a deep breath, then strutted, in character, to the area in front of the garage door where there were no instruments or sleeping bags and began her comedy routine.

Naomi, Maren, and Katherine laughed until their sides hurt. Bridget was insanely funny. And it wasn't just what she said, it was the *way* she said it, with just the right pauses and facial expressions and gestures. She was really good, and her stage presence had definitely improved since fourth grade. The only problem was that, at six minutes, it was still way too long for the show. So, for the better part of the next hour, she ran shorter bits as her friends critiqued and cut and condensed, successfully bringing it down to a tight four.

Maren said she'd go next. She hadn't planned to dance tonight—her routines usually required a bigger stage—but her friends insisted, and she finally gave in. She had been thinking of doing her jazz routine, but it definitely needed more space. So she decided to go ahead with the tap number she'd originally planned—it would be easier to adapt to the small room. Actually, it was a tap dance without the taps, since her shoes were at home, which was just as well because taps are notoriously loud, and Katherine's family was sound asleep.

Cuing up her song, she handed her phone to Naomi and took up her starting position. Standing totally still for a few moments, it looked like her eyes were closed. Then, lifting her head gracefully, she nodded to Naomi to press *play*.

Wow, she was talented!

As she quietly tapped onto the imaginary stage with impeccable posture and carefully choreographed movements, Maren looked like a different person. She wore no stage make-up or costume, but had somehow undergone an invisible transformation. It was the first time Katherine noticed that Maren's dancing was about so much more than her feet. Her face and arms and body were a big part of it, too. And although Katherine was well aware of how hard Maren worked at her craft, in the polished performance you couldn't tell. It looked effortless. She was going to be a star.

With no band present, Katherine gave a pass on a sneak-peek tonight, but instead invited her friends to come hear them tomorrow after the shirts were done.

"What if we bring shirts and dye them, too?" Bridget asked.

"I was thinking the same thing!" added Naomi. "We could be like roadies or groupies—you know, 'hanging with the band'." Maren nodded enthusiastically.

"I love it!" said Katherine, hoping that her bandmates would agree. "I'll text in the morning about colors and stuff, 'cause we're trying to coordinate."

With their energy spent, the girls sneaked into the kitchen for the remaining brownies, settled into sleeping bags, and put their favorite movie on to play one more time. Its themes of dancing and friends and fun swirled in Katherine's mind as she fell asleep thinking of her own friends and their closed-eye transformation into performers.

CHAPTER SIXTEEN
THE WORLDS ALIGNED
SUNDAY

Sunday's tie-dye party was about the most fun Katherine had had doing any kind of craft ever. And she enjoyed crafts. They were the one thing that made summer camp tolerable. Although, in fairness, tie-dying might be closer to an *art* than a *craft,* what with all of the creative possibilities it held. This probably explained how happy she felt. Or, more likely, her joy had to do with the fact that her worlds were colliding, or perhaps aligning, in the best possible way.

It turned out that the girls all sort-of kind-of knew each other. They'd never been what you would call *friends,* but they had been in classes, groups, or teams together. And over white shirts, buckets of dye, and a mountain of rubber bands, they found they were remarkably compatible. It was a relief, if Katherine was being honest, even if she hadn't fully formed a concern before this moment. Bridget, Naomi, and Maren were her best friends—they had been forever. But Charlotte, Aaliyah, and Mariana had become important to her lately, too. Knowing that her two worlds got along made life better and easier.

Thanks to some mid-morning group texting, six boxes of dye were brought to the table: purple, magenta, green, yellow, red, and blue, which would form the palette for the shirts. Everyone agreed to use at least a little of each color in its pure form before branching into blends. With the giant pile of rubber bands divided among them, the girls tightly wrapped a zillion parts of the shirts in hopes of landing on some cool designs. They tried to imagine the patterns that would result, but tie-dye always surprised.

Figuring that any spills would only add to the garage's vibe, they did the coloring inside. Katherine's family had a long folding table stored in the garage for big events, and they set it up in front of the door. Her mom always covered it with a fancy tablecloth, so they didn't have to be too careful with the dye, but they used an old plastic cloth anyway and found that it's festive balloon images only added to the party atmosphere. When the six five-gallon pails were filled halfway (in the utility sink—a bonus garage feature), the girls began carefully mixing colors using the giant stir sticks that Mr. Keyes kept in his painting supplies.

Meticulously securing the bands and dipping small sections of the shirts carefully in just the right amount of color, the girls tried to imagine how they would look once untied. It was hard to wait for the shirts to dry before peeking under the bands, but they knew that would just mess things up. Still, they all had active imaginations and gushingly praised each other's work as they finished up.

Bridget, Aaliyah, and Mariana were psyched about having full-on groupies, and they felt it only appropriate to give them a sneak peek of their song. Excited, Bridget, Maren, and Naomi pulled spare crates from a shelf and arranged them in the driveway, leaving a space between the 'stage' and the audience. It was strange, Katherine realized, but she didn't feel her usual anxiety—just a tingle of excitement. Although she had always kept her music life rather private, she found that she really wanted to share this band experience with her friends. They had been so happy for her when she first told them about it, and had jumped on board as groupies—it made her heart swell. Hopefully, they'd like what they heard.

It turned out that *like* was an understatement.

They *LOVED* it!

"Oh my gosh," said Bridget. "You guys are amazing! You are so going to blow everyone away!"

"Just—wow!" added Naomi.

"So impressive. Seriously—you are really, really good," Maren smiled, looking her friend directly in the eyes.

Katherine beamed. Their first, albeit informal, performance for an audience, had felt awesome. *Would it feel like this when they played for a bigger crowd?* The hint of a knot in her stomach said it wasn't likely. And she knew in her heart that playing for her three best friends couldn't compare to performing for hundreds of students, teachers, and parents. She pushed the thought aside and focused on the joy of the moment.

Katherine knew the audience was biased. Of course they were. But she also knew her friends well enough to tell when they were simply being kind, and right now what she saw on their faces was real admiration. Her thoughts were confirmed a moment later.

"Can you play it again?"

CHAPTER SEVENTEEN
THE SURPRISE
MONDAY

For the second week in a row, Katherine found herself standing in front of Mrs. Bellamy's door with some trepidation. She hadn't practiced anywhere near her normal amount since the audition. A pang of guilt washed over her when Mrs. Bellamy greeted her at the door like a friend she'd been waiting all week to see. Katherine felt conspicuous. She didn't think she could fake her way through the lesson.

"I, uh, haven't practiced very much this week…" she said hesitantly as they moved into the piano room. "I mean, I've been *playing*, just not my repertoire." Sheepishly she added, "I, uh… joined a rock band."

Katherine hadn't planned on sharing this news today, it just came out, and she braced herself for her teacher's response. But of all the possibilities growing in her imagination, what came next wasn't one of them.

"A rock band—how wonderful!" Mrs. Bellamy exclaimed, her eyes smiling. "And you're playing the piano?"

"Yes—I mean, keyboard..." Katherine stuttered, recovering from the shock.

"Fantastic! And are you learning from sheet music or from recordings?"

Katherine didn't know there *were* scores for rock songs—she'd have to look into it. "From the recordings," she said. "It takes a little longer, but not too much—mostly it just took some getting used to."

"That's those wonderful aural skills you've developed—useful, aren't they?" she said in a teasing voice. Katherine had not enjoyed ear training, but she remembered her teacher's long-ago words: *It's a pain now, Katherine, I know, but you'll find them helpful one day.*

"Do you want to play for me? I'd love to hear what you've been working on!"

Katherine played through each of the band's songs, and Mrs. Bellamy told her she was so impressed with what she had done. "You know, it's no small thing to be able to learn from a recording. Your ears are serving you well! Great work!"

"Thanks," she smiled proudly. "I was a little nervous at first. I mean, I didn't *mean* to join a band. It just kind of happened. But I like it... the music is fun." She paused for a moment. "And I really like being part of something bigger than just me and my instrument, you know? As something extra, I mean—I still love playing my classical pieces, too." And she realized for the first time in weeks that this was, in fact, true.

"I *do* know, Katherine. It's really special to be able to make music with a group *and* on your own. I'm so happy for you!"

Mrs. Bellamy went to the bookshelf that was home to her zillions of music books. Katherine had seen her do it many times before and assumed she was selecting a new piece for her to try. But she came back with something unexpected. A photo album. She opened the book and turned a few yellow-tinged pages until she found the one she was looking for—an old picture of a small band on stage. The fashions dated it as much as the faded colors did. It must have been 20 or 30 years old. Mrs. Bellamy stared at the image with far-off eyes. And as Katherine took in the scene, too, her gaze turned to a girl by the keyboard. She couldn't have been more than 16. The twinkling eyes and kind smile were so familiar.

"This was *my* band, Katherine. I was just a little older than you when we started. We performed for more than 10 years!"

"Wow!" said Katherine, shocked to her core. It had never occurred to her that her Mozart-Bach-and-Beethoven-loving piano teacher had any interest in any other style of music, but the guitars and drums told a different story.

"What kind of music did you play?" she asked.

"Light rock, folk, a little bit of country—it kind of depended on the audience we were playing for."

"Do you still play? What happened to your band?"

"I do still play that music, sometimes. And sometimes I play Beethoven. It really depends on how I feel and who I'm with. A musician is a *musician*, you know? And there is a world of music out there. Why should we have to stick to only style?"

She sat back, reflecting, "As for my band... we performed quite a lot—all through high school and university, and even afterward. But it wasn't the career that all of my bandmates wanted in the end. They went on to do other things. I'm the only one who stayed with music full-time—there was never anything else for me," she said with a smile. "We still see each other from time to time—and we usually play together when we do. It's still fun, even after all these years." Looking directly at Katherine, she said, "I'm glad you have this in your life now."

"Do you think you could teach me some of those styles?"

"You, know, I think you've already taught yourself quite a lot. But I'd love to teach you what I know. Your usual repertoire can wait another week!" And with that, the lesson Katherine had been dreading turned out to be one of her best ever.

***

When dinner was done and the dishes cleared, she found herself drawn to the piano for the first time in weeks. Opening the cover, she ran her fingers gently along the keys. Then, lifting the lid onto the tall peg, she sat down, closed her eyes, and breathed deeply in and out. In the aftermath of an extraordinary lesson, the music came to her and her heart was at home.

Katherine hadn't felt this way or played this way in ages. As she focused on the feel of the keys beneath her fingers and the sounds they were creating, all the tension and avoidance of the last few weeks was released. Her old pieces found new life and her love for them was rekindled.

Katherine's world had changed—it fell apart and then pieced itself together in the most unexpected ways. Strangely, she felt more secure and more confident, in herself and in her music, than she ever had before. New friends and contexts and styles that moved her away from what she had known and where she had been was, it seemed, exactly what she'd needed to find her way back. The fateful audition felt distant, and she was okay— better than okay—which she never thought she would be again.

CHAPTER EIGHTEEN
THE AUDITION
TUESDAY

It was audition day. And in spite of the realizations and revelations of late, Katherine's stomach was in a knot and she wasn't sure she could do it. Stuffing her unbanded shirt into her backpack, she dressed on autopilot, determined not to think or to panic.

"Good luck today!" her Mom called out as she pulled into the drop-off zone. "Remember to have fun!"

"Thanks, Mom," she answered, her voice tight. "I'll try." Katherine managed a weak smile as her mom's words echoed in her ears. The weekend had been a lot of fun, and the band did sound awesome. Still, the knot refused to budge.

At lunchtime, the band, along with Naomi, Bridget, and Maren, met for one last run-through. They ran the song twice and, feeling good about how it sounded, made a plan for after school while grabbing a quick bite. Her friends *oohed* and *aahed* over the cool patterns on their shirts. Surrounded by so much excitement, Katherine couldn't bring herself to pull out, so instead she stayed quiet and tried to participate in the conversation at least with nods and smiles and other vague looks of engagement.

It was Naomi who first noticed Katherine's silence. "Everything okay, Katherine?" she asked.

But Katherine didn't hear her. Her mind was too full of her own doubts and worries.

The girls exchanged curious looks.

"Kat?" Maren chimed in.

Katherine snapped back to the moment. "Yeah?"

"Um…" said Maren, "Are you okay?"

"Yeah—why do you ask?"

"You're just kind of quiet. And a little pale."

"Oh." Katherine couldn't think of a better response.

Now everyone was quiet. Charlotte broke the silence. "Are you worried about the audition?"

Katherine wasn't sure what to say. "Well, not worried, exactly," she said after a moment.

"Are you anxious about it?" asked Maren in a calm and knowing voice.

Katherine froze. She had never talked about her stage fright with anyone. Ever.

"A little, I guess," she said in a small voice. "Sorry."

Aaliyah looked at her curiously. "Why are you sorry? You played great just now." She smiled and added, "Everyone gets a little nervous before they perform."

Katherine looked around at her friends. None of them looked nervous at all. "I don't know…" she said. "You guys don't seem very nervous."

"Oh, I've got butterflies," said Bridget. "Are you kidding? Total butterflies. Like, since I signed up!"

"Me too," added Mariana. "I hardly slept last night. And when I did, I kept dreaming that something went wrong. First, I lost my drumsticks. Then I hit the drum too hard and smashed a hole in it. And just before I woke up, the sticks slipped out of my hands completely, flew into the audience, and hit Mr. Ryan in the head!"

Everyone laughed.

"We sound great, Kat," said Charlotte. "You've got to remember that. Just focus on how it feels when we play. Let the music and excitement kind of run through you. You're a great musician! Think of the butterflies as fuel to power you through."

Maren was quiet. She looked deep in thought, and Katherine wondered what about. The most experienced performer of them all—by a long shot—she was always *so* together and *so* calm and *so very good*. Katherine wondered now if she ever felt nervous or unsure. It certainly didn't seem like it.

As if sensing her thoughts, Maren's far-away gaze shifted, and she looked in Katherine's eyes. "You know I do a mental run-through, right? I think I mentioned it before? I wonder if it might work for you, too? You know—help you focus. I can show you how..."

***

Katherine waited on the front steps with Maren for her Mom to pick her up. The others had all headed off already, but

Katherine had promised her mom that she'd help with a grocery run, so she was picking her up along the way. Maren had a rehearsal shortly, so she, too, was waiting for a ride. Raiding the stash of snacks she kept for nights when there was no time to go home, they sat on the steps together, enjoying the quiet of the evening air.

"What did you think about the audition?" Maren asked nonchalantly. "Did the visualization help?"

"It did actually," said Katherine. "I mean, *I think* it went well. I was nervous, but I was able to focus better than I usually do."

"Yeah, I find it just kind of gets me into the zone, you know?"

Katherine wondered if simply talking with her friends about her anxieties, and hearing that they had them, too, was what helped her more than anything. But whatever it was that did it, she was able to get through the audition reasonably confidently and the judges seemed to respond well. She felt relieved and exhausted and a million times better than she had a few hours earlier.

"Maren," Katherine asked cautiously, "why aren't you going to *Valley View* next year? You're so much more polished and professional than me, and they have a great dance program—but you've never mentioned any interest in it. How come?" It was a risk, mentioning the school, but Katherine felt she might just be okay now to talk about the audition, and she really wanted to know what was up with her talented friend.

Maren was quiet for a moment; she looked at her feet. "So… I was offered a job."

A job? What kind of job? She waited for Maren to continue.

"Like, with a dance company. A professional one."

"Oh," Katherine's eyes were wide and her jaw dropped open.

"And I accepted it. Which means I'll be touring next year. I'll have to go to school virtually instead of in person."

"Wow…" was all she could think of to say for a moment. "That's amazing! I mean, I'm not surprised—well, I *am* surprised, but I'm also not surprised." She paused before asking, "Why didn't you tell us?"

"I guess I just wanted to be sure about it first. I think I needed time to decide what I really wanted to do without having to talk about it or hear what other people thought about it. My parents are the only ones who know—well, besides you now."

"I get that—I mean, not wanting to talk about it. I probably would have done the same thing. I kind of wish no one had known about my *Valley View* audition." Katherine was shocked to find herself bringing it up.

"Did something happen there?" Maren asked gently. "I noticed you haven't said anything about it, but I didn't want to pry. It didn't go well?"

Katherine took a deep breath in and slowly exhaled. With her gaze focused squarely on the passing cars, she quietly told her story. "No, it didn't go well…" She paused and took another deep breath before going on. "I blanked. I mean I *totally* blanked. Everything seemed to be going really well… And I was thinking about how well it was going and what a relief it was… I was almost at the end. And then I lost my place. I just blanked. I couldn't find my notes."

Maren's voice was sympathetic, "What did you do?"

Katherine shook her head, remembering the panicked moment. "I jumped to a starting place. It was the only thing I could think to do."

Seeing the question mark on her friend's face, she explained, "Mrs. Bellamy had me practice all of these points I could jump to if I ever ran into trouble. And this was one of those moments. I had to leave out, like, half a page—in a piece that everyone knows and is impossible to hide in." Katherine closed her eyes for a moment before continuing. "So I jumped to a starting point, finished the piece, and tried to pretend that nothing had happened. But I still had to play one more piece! I don't even remember how that one went. I just felt like such a fraud, smiling and bowing and walking offstage as if it had all gone great."

Maren looked at her with a curious smile. "Kat," she said, "I get why you're upset; I mean that's stressful. But honestly—and I'm not just saying this to make you feel better—honestly, that's pretty amazing. I mean, how you handled yourself sounds pretty professional to me."

Katherine turned to look at her friend for the first time since beginning the story. She shook her head sadly, "No, Maren. The competition to get into this school is so tough." And as she said it, the image of red velvet curtains flashed before her eyes and she was reminded painfully of how at home she had felt there. "I totally messed up."

"Yeah, okay. But then you picked yourself up and kept going, and you didn't fall apart. That's what I'm talking about. It's exactly what my dance teacher always tells us—mistakes happen to everyone, it's what you do in the moment that distinguishes between a successful performance and a failure. And, Kat, it sounds like you succeeded."

CHAPTER NINETEEN
THE TEAR JERKERS
WEDNESDAY AND THURSDAY

The baby robins were awake and hungry. Their little beaks poked up out of the nest, opening and closing in the hope that their Mama would soon drop some worms into them. The weather was getting warmer and the days longer as sixth grade inched toward summer. There was a new life in the air that only the end of a long school year could bring. It probably helped that there was *actual* new life all around, from the tiny leaves to the blooming buds to the baby birds. But as awesome as this all was, nothing could compare to the fact that school was coming to a close.

And just as the rest of school life seemed to be slowing down, the music department was ramping up. The end of the year brought graduation and concerts and assemblies, in addition to the much-anticipated talent show—which, in Katherine's opinion, was really a *music* showcase with a few side acts—

though she wouldn't frame it that way to Bridget and Maren, whose investment in their respective arts was impressive.

Students in each of the school ensembles spent much of the next three days in rehearsals. Normally relegated to one block per week of *official* school time and one lunch rehearsal, as the end-of-year closed in, Mrs. Gibbons and Mr. Bertulli had free reign to bring their groups together as much as they needed to prepare for these important events. Although Music as a subject area wasn't always given the academic respect that Katherine and her bandmates felt it deserved, no one could deny that it was *music* that made a school gathering come to life.

On Wednesday, Thursday, and Friday, Katherine's mornings were divided between the band room, choir room, and auditorium. *And she loved it.* This was the way life, *her* life, should be. And there was a tiny piece of her that still hoped it could be. But regardless of what Mrs. Bellamy and Maren said, she felt that the wish was futile. She would be better off accepting the more realistic prospect of serving out her school days with her friends in the regular public schools. It wasn't such a bad image. It just wasn't what she had imagined.

And then she was off again, thinking about what could be— correction: *what could have been*—if only she had kept it together. She dreamed about days spent surrounded by musicians and dancers and actors, all collaborating and learning from each other. About hallways filled with musical sounds and teachers who *got it*.

For all the joy that music brought to every aspect of life, it seemed to Katherine that so few people—so few adults, anyway— really *got* how important it was. She simply couldn't imagine what she would do without music—and would happily trade all of her school classes in a heartbeat for one more instrument or song or opportunity to learn music.

The choral song she was playing was coming along beautifully. It was tricky, no doubt, but Katherine relished the complexity, and marrying it together with the voices was exhilarating. She marveled at how composers came up with such ideas for sound combinations—*just thought them up*! Out of silence, they created masterful collections of sounds that could transport you to another dimension. *Had a musical dimension ever been defined before?* Surely it had…

In band, the usual *Pomp and Circumstance* was rehearsed *ad nauseum* until the students could play it in their sleep. The notes were easy enough, but playing it at a perfectly steady tempo and avoiding the temptation to speed it all up a bit was a challenge. It was cheesy, Katherine knew, but she loved the way the music swelled as the pitch moved higher and rounded the climax. She could almost see the students—her friends—marching in their caps and gowns, ready to take on the next big challenge that was junior high. They played the song over and over on a loop, as they would at graduation, so that Katherine and the other graduating band members could practice laying down their instruments at different intervals to walk across the stage when their names were called.

The choir sang a couple of tear-jerkers, one directed at the students and another at parents. *You know* —the usual *'I'll never forget you/I'll always be here for you'* and the *'I'd never have made it here without you'* fare that featured prominently in graduation ceremonies everywhere. And since Katherine didn't sing in the choir, she sat back listening, and teared up on cue at both. Partly, it was the meaning in the words and partly the poignancy in the music itself, but the songs made her think about her friends and family who had indeed been there for her always, supporting her dreams, and never failing to boost her up, no matter how sick to death they were of hearing the same pieces practiced over and over again. Even Declan, who she was pretty sure could live happily without ever seeing or hearing a piano again, never complained about her practicing at all hours and claiming the nicest room in the house for herself and her instrument.

Her mom and dad had been her true champions, though she rarely thought it, much less stated it. She was so grateful to have them for parents. What would she have done if they were the type who felt that music was a fun-but-not-realistic path—that she should become a lawyer or accountant or doctor? *Ugh.* Great careers, she had no doubt, but definitely not for her. No, her parents knew *who* she was and *what* she was, and they supported her artistic growth in every way imaginable, from keeping her stocked in paints and canvases to offering up the living room and garage as rehearsal space, to buying her a beautiful and expensive piano with funds that they got from who-knows-where. How interesting that she never felt pressure from them to succeed or be the best. *Only ever support.*

Katherine was lucky. She knew it, and these stupid tear-jerkers confirmed it for her. She owed mom and dad a hug.

CHAPTER TWENTY
THE TALENT SHOW
FRIDAY

Although it had only been a couple of weeks since the talent show was announced, Katherine and her friends felt like they had been waiting forever. Finally, the big day was here! The show started at 7pm, but the dress rehearsal began right after school and the band room wasn't available at lunchtime, so another run through was out of the question. This was it! Katherine and the band met on the school steps as soon as the end-of-day bell rang, and together they made their way to the auditorium. Scanning the order of performances posted on the door, they found their names at the bottom. *The very bottom.*

They were last?

Charlotte screamed in excitement. "This is amazing!" she exclaimed. "Our first performance and we get to close the show!"

"What? Like, so this is good?" Mariana's confused query echoed Katherine's thoughts.

"Are you kidding? This is fantastic!" Charlotte responded. "They must have really liked our audition!" Every show keeps the best performance for last—you know, to end on a high note."

Katherine felt the butterflies flutter in her stomach. *Breathe*, she told herself. Just *breathe*.

The only trouble with being last was that the dress rehearsal was going to run much later for them than anticipated. There would only be an hour or so between the end of rehearsal and the start of the show—barely enough time to get home, changed, and back again. They decided to stay put and order pizza.

The dress rehearsal was actually a lot of fun. They got to hear all the other performers—literally *ALL* of them—which they wouldn't get to do that night. So much talent! And a few wishful thinkers... but mostly a lot of talent. There were several other bands, some soloists, a couple of gymnasts, a couple of dance groups, Maren's beautiful solo, Bridget's stand-up routine, a juggling act, a couple of comedy sketches, one lip sync performance, and a surprisingly good magician. All kinds of kids had come out—the ones you totally expected and the ones you never dreamed of. Katherine found that to be the most interesting part of all, the kids with hidden talents—seemingly ordinary kids with talented alter egos. She guessed there would be a lot of people surprised to see her up there tonight and not behind a piano by herself. She caught her breath again.

Finally, it was their turn. It was dinnertime already and the girls figured the room would be empty. They figured wrong. Almost all the performers had stuck around until the end, and all eyes were on the stage. Katherine set up her keyboard quickly. Mariana was using the school drums and, while she adjusted them and Aaliyah and Charlotte tuned, Katherine closed her eyes and pictured her happy place—her lovely garage. Breathing in and out purposefully and deeply, she let the good vibes of her bandmates and friends wash over her. They could hear Maren and Naomi and Bridget hooting and cheering them on. Katherine felt exhilarated.

And then they began, excitement and music flooding their veins, playing through to the end without missing a beat. The applause was thunderous! It felt great!

Of course, Katherine reminded herself, this was only the dress rehearsal; there would be 20 times as many people in the audience tonight. But still—a win was a win. And this felt like one.

Maren and Bridget joined the band for pizza—in the band room, where they had first connected. Even Naomi was able to sneak away from her crew duties for a few minutes to join them. The girls chatted and laughed, old friends and new, still on a high from which they were unlikely to come down until well after the show had ended.

***

The choir and band rooms were designated official *green rooms*, so by 6:45, the room was full. Katherine finally understood why they were labelled *green*—she was feeling a little queasy herself—but, if she was being honest, much less so than she usually did. The dress rehearsal helped, and so did hanging out and having fun with her bandmates and friends. Beyond preparation, breathing strategies, and mental run-throughs,

106

there was something to be said for plain old distraction.

Mr. Aronson, the drama teacher, came in a few minutes later to wish everyone well and to give a run-down of the evening's proceedings. *The show would start in 10 minutes, at 7pm on the dot. Intermission would take place at approximately 8:15. Performers would be called out by a crew member three acts before their own, so they'd be ready backstage when it was their turn.* And he reminded them that sometimes order changes had to be made on the fly, so it was possible that they could go on a little ahead or behind where they were in the current order.

The students took it all in, and by the time he left there were only a few minutes remaining before showtime. The energy in the room was palpable. Katherine paused for a brief moment, suddenly aware that she was, indeed, *excited.* Not so much anxious or nervous, but actually excited, with only a tinge of those other feelings. *Hmmm... this was new.* She hoped it would last.

Soon things were underway. Maren was in the first half, and her friends wished they could sneak out to see her, but they had been warned by Mr. Aronson that the house was full, so there would be no room for performers to watch. The live feed to the room was helpful, but the screen was small and the image grainy. Still, it was better than nothing, and they watched breathlessly as Maren glided onto the stage, took her position, and moved flawlessly through her routine. She returned to the room minutes after her performance with eyes and smile bright. Her demeanor was so poised and professional, and Katherine was struck once again by the news that she would be leaving them soon. *To work as a professional!* She simultaneously found it hard to wrap her head around and impossible not to see this as an inevitable outcome for her beautiful friend.

At Intermission, the band changed into their performance shirts. There were still about 40 minutes to go before they'd be called backstage, but it seemed like the right thing to do at the official break. Katherine's mom had starched and ironed the whole lot of them, so in addition to looking fresh and hip, they also looked crisp and stage-ready—an interesting combination that seemed to work somehow.

One million selfies and group shots later, the band turned to the business of why they were there. *To perform.* Katherine felt the butterflies flicker, but she thought of her friends and their sage words, "Everyone gets butterflies before they perform. Think of them as fuel." She decisively told herself:

This is normal.

Everyone has them.

Use them!

She remembered watching Maren and Bridget getting ready to perform at the sleepover—closing their eyes and breathing deeply. Katherine channeled her friends. Closing her eyes, she filled her lungs, breathing in slowly and deeply. She could feel the air filling her whole body, pushing out her core, and having a curiously steadying effect on her nerves. She released the air in a slow, even stream, then breathed in again.

Feeling significantly more grounded, Katherine turned her attention to her bandmates. Charlotte was pulling up the audio from their Sunday run-through. They moved to a corner away from the rest of the performers and huddled around her phone to listen. Hearing their song was exactly what Katherine needed. She could feel the music deep in her soul—and she remembered why she did this: *Because she had to*. Music was part of who she was. A *big* part. And her need to make music fueled her desire to share it—to perform it. A lightbulb went off inside Katherine's head. *Performing was not about her!* Not exactly, anyway. It was about the audience—sharing the music with them!

This was a massive revelation for 9pm on a Friday and Katherine's mind was floating. She felt like she had taken a quantum leap. But there was no more time to process right now—there was a performance to give. Katherine kept her epiphany to herself, tucking it carefully close to her chest and making a silent vow to never forget it. As Charlotte and Aaliyah turned to tuning their instruments and Mariana collected her sticks, brushes, and cowbell, Katherine sat back and closed her eyes again. This time she played it all through in her mind. *Leaving the green room to walk backstage. Watching the kids onstage from behind the curtain. Hearing their act called. Heading onstage. Listening to the cheers. Standing behind her keyboard. Seeing the stage lights above. Starting to play. Becoming one with her bandmates. Making great music. Feeling the joy from the crowd. Feeling the joy inside.*

Katherine walked onstage with butterflies dancing energetically to the music inside her. She was nervous and excited and alert and happy. *Who knew you could have all of these feelings at once?* Determinedly, she told herself *those butterflies are fuel*, as she willed them to energize her focus. And as the band started to play and sing, she thought only of the swell of sound that was washing over her, from within her, from around her. A sound that soon included cheering and clapping and tapping along from a swarm of joyful fans. It was infectious and glorious, and she loved every minute of it. Katherine looked around at her bandmates. Charlotte and Aaliyah and Mariana were in her sound bubble, too, she could see, rocking out as the music rose up from them. It was magical and awesome. And, as Katherine learned that night, awesome beats perfect, every time.

POSTLUDE

THE BEGINNING

FRIDAY

Katherine said goodbye to the last of her friends at 11:30pm. The after-party—in the garage, of course—had been so much fun. Full of laughter and joy and food and, of course, music. Best day ever! She closed the garage door and headed inside. As she turned out the lights, she looked back at her practice space. *What a difference a few weeks make*, she thought.

Shaking her head slightly, it was a little hard to believe this was her life. *That this was her. In a rock band! With its first fantastic performance!* And most surprising of all was that this whole thing had happened in the aftermath of the worst performance she had ever given. She shook her head again.

Katherine supposed it could all be a dream, but she didn't think so. It seemed pretty real, as much as it also seemed *surreal*. *Could those two words be used in the same sentence?* She was too tired to think about it.

As she made her way through the kitchen on route to her room, Katherine stopped for a glass of water and one more tiny cupcake, an admitted weakness. She sat down in a happy, fuzzy, wired-but-tired haze while removing the little paper wrapper. As her teeth sunk into the buttery goodness something caught her eye. An envelope. Just an ordinary envelope, but there was something familiar about it…

Oh. Her name was on it.

Her name was on it?

She was tired. She blinked and looked away, then looked back again. Yes, it was definitely addressed to her. *Okay. So, she never got mail—like, ever…*

Katherine reached out to pick it up. She looked at her name up close and then at the return address. Her breath caught in her chest. *Valley View School for the Performing Arts.* Staring at it for a moment, she tried to decide what to do. She had been waiting for this letter her whole life—or at least it felt that way. But now that it was here, she wasn't sure she wanted it. 'We regret to inform you…' would definitely put a damper on the best day ever. She laid it back down and headed up the stairs. Bad news could wait until tomorrow.

Except that tomorrow refused to come. Katherine couldn't sleep. Her imagination was running wild, making rest impossible, in spite of her exhaustion. And after an hour or so, she gave in and made her way slowly back down the stairs. Her mom was in the kitchen making tea.

"Hi Sweetie," she said with a smile, "I thought you were sleeping."

"I thought I would be, too, but I couldn't get to sleep." Her eyes drifted toward the envelope.

Her mom smiled, delighted, "Well, I'm glad you're up. I could use some company. Would you like some tea?"

Mom poured, while Katherine put the milk and sugar on the table. They sat down and prepared their tea quietly together.

"So, you had quite a day," Mom said. "Your first rock band performance!"

"Yeah," she said in a far-off voice.

They sat in silence for a minute or two, unready to acknowledge the elephant they both knew was in the room.

Mrs. Keyes gently, almost imperceptibly, nodded toward the envelope, "Do you want to open it?"

Katherine looked up at her, uncertainty filling her eyes. "No," she said, followed moments later by a deep breath and, "Yes. But…"

Mrs. Keyes put her hand on top of Katherine's and looked in her eyes. "Katherine, you have so much going for you. You are a beautiful musician and a beautiful person. You are *so very talented*. No matter what this letter says, *that will not change*." She paused before adding, "And, for the record, I thought your audition was excellent (full disclosure: I did have my ear to the door)."

Katherine smiled at this image. Staring at the envelope a moment longer, she reached out to pick it up. She picked at the corner of the flap and pulled a little piece off. Then another and another, until it was open. Pulling its contents out cautiously, she unfolded the letter and her eyes filled with tears as she read:

Dear Ms. Keyes,

Thank you for considering Valley View School for the Performing Arts as the next step in your performance training. The admissions committee was pleased to meet you and to hear you perform.

In addition to your high level of skill and musicianship, they were especially impressed with your stage presence and grace in the face of obstacles, with one faculty member noting "… while every musician experiences moments when things do not go as intended on stage, Ms. Keyes showed an adeptness for navigating the moment smoothly and skillfully so as to not detract from the excellence of the music she was creating. I dare say that an untrained listener would not have known that anything had gone awry."

This, together with outstanding test scores, have earned you a place in next year's entering class, should you wish to join us. Congratulations! We hope that you will accept this offer…"

Katherine's jaw dropped in disbelief, and she read the letter again to make sure that she understood. *She did. She was in!*

She looked up and saw her mom smiling that big, proud smile that only she could make. Her mom, who was always there, supporting and encouraging and championing her—who, at this moment, Katherine realized, was quietly giving her the moment she needed to process, waiting for her to speak.

But there were so many thoughts, all jumbled on top of each other. Words wouldn't come. So Katherine responded in the only way she could, as she wrapped her arms tightly around her mom.

In a silence that resembled the end of a great musical experience, they held each other for a long time—and dreamed of the one that was about to begin.

Charlene A. Ryan is an author, educator, musician, painter, and mom. She has spent most of her life behind an instrument and in front of an audience of one kind or another.

To learn more about Charlene, her work and other books, visit charlenearyan.com